MOTION PICTURE
DISTRIBUTION HANDBOOK

Other TAB Books by the Author:

No. 1115
$19.95

MOTION PICTURE DISTRIBUTION HANDBOOK

BY JOSEPH F. ROBERTSON

TAB BOOKS Inc.
BLUE RIDGE SUMMIT, PA. 17214

FIRST EDITION

FIRST PRINTING

Copyright © 1981 by TAB BOOKS Inc.

Printed in the United States of America

Library of Congress Cataloging in Publication Data

Robertson, Joseph F
    Motion picture distribution handbook.

    Includes index.
    1. Moving-pictures—United States—Distribution.
I. Title.
PN1994.A2R56   791.43'0973   79-14531
ISBN 0-8306-9797-7

Contents

Preface

You are about to embark on a journey which takes you through the maze of mystery surrounding motion picture distribution.

Most of you are in the motion picture industry or will be in the future. Some of you could make that . . . great American film. Maybe, you might inadvertently place that precious work of love in the hands of an unfeeling and totally objective businessman called *a motion picture distributor*. A good one can make you a fortune—and there are some good ones. A bad one can steal that fortune.

In law, the term *caveat emptor* is used extensively. This term, *let the buyer beware* can also be applied to the motion picture producer. The motion picture industry is a loose industry built upon trust. However, one would be foolish to assume that all people in the industry are honest. Some are not! In this book, we show you how to avoid tempting the distributor, the theatres, the sub-distributors and last but not least, the employees.

On the positive end, this book teaches you all the hidden secrets of distribution. It is an accumulation of knowledge gained through actual experience and trial and error.

The distribution industry is traditionally closed mouthed. Its procedures are guarded, and many of the executives go out of their way to make the jargon incomprehensible.

This book enables the reader to conceptually understand the industry. If the reader is fully focused, he will be one of the chosen few because 99% of the people in the industry still do not understand.

Study this book and have the courage to grow from the knowledge gained. Success lies within yourself.

Joseph F. Robertson

Dedication

TO:

Shel Haimes ....who kept suggesting new chapters. I hated him.
Ken Snyder ....who liked everything I wrote. I liked him.
David Lyon .... who helped keep the book in the English Language.
Mira Stewart ....who made me Iced Tea.
Alfred Choy ....my friend. We both learned motion picture "biz".
All exchanges.......................who taught me how one can steal.
Major Distributors ....whose indifference motivated this book.

He who seeks truth . . .
and does not compromise . . .
is not the oppressor!

Nor is he the oppressed . . .
for he is above these things!
He is free.

Verite!
Nothing can destroy you.

To seek truth . . .
One must begin!

Chapter 1
Demographics

Demo, from the Greek language, means people. Demo combined with the French word, *Graphie*, means the statistical study of human populations, especially with reference to size and density, distribution and vital statistics. Primarily, motion picture distributors use demographics to study theatre audiences by age group.

For example, in the 1960s and 1970s, the bulk of theatre-going audiences were in the 18 to 30-year-old bracket. Table 1-1 shows the percentage of theatre participation of the total 100 percent theatre-going audience.

There are approximately 73,000,000 people over 40 years old in the United States. However, one cannot consider all of these people as theatre-going audiences. Only six percent of this population are theatre going. Many people make the mistake of looking at the total population and then estimating that all of the people in the population are theatre going. They are not!

There are different environmental emotions between age groups. The 18 to 30 year olds do not respond to love situations or fearful situations in the same way as the 40 year olds and older respond to the same situation.

That is what the generation gap is all about. Generation gap, or lag, is based on the environmental backgrounds of the different generations. Older people, raised in the bleak depression years, react quite differently than younger people raised in affluent and inflationary periods.

Table 1-1. Audience Attendance at the Theatre.

Percent Attending	Age Group
87%	18 to 30-years-old
7%	below 18-years-old
5%	between 30 and 40-years-old
1%	over 50-years-old

Future Shock also enters the picture. Since the end of World War II, advances in technology and general knowledge have increased faster and faster. Each five year period triples the preceding five year period. Many older people, as well as some 18 to 30 year olds, drop out of this whirling vortex, and are not exposed (either voluntarily or involuntarily) to this fast-paced world. If they drop out for more than two years, it will be almost impossible for them to catch up with the world. Occasionally, we see a motion picture with an *ageless concept* appealing to all age audiences. This is extremely rare. Many films made with older people in the cast aren't necessarily for older viewing audiences, but rather for the 18 to 30 year old group.

One cannot take a chance of trying to make an *ageless* film. Many people over 40 are the producers and distributors of motion pictures. They are the 'power' in Hollywood and, sometimes, they make films for themselves. Their sense of humor and dialogue is totally foreign to the younger groups. Since the younger group makes up 87 percent of the theatre audiences, the film is a total flop. These same producers and distributors do not go to the movies, and yet they call the shots on what is to be distributed. Ironic, isn't it? Many times, these powerful men go so far as to use an aging, worn-out sex-symbol as a vamp. It is not only comical but also totally unbelievable and unrealistic to this age group.

A much deeper demographic study can be made to evaluate audiences by income group, metro, urban or rural, white collar, blue collar or no collar. These enlarged demographics can be used as a tool to study theatre-going results in many areas. One can combine economics, attitudes, moods, environments, dress, customs, religious beliefs, etc.

PENDULUM OR CYCLICAL THEORY

Pendulum, or *cyclical theory* is a statistical technique used in the motion picture industry to show that at any given time, the western genre, or mystery film, or science-fiction film, etc. will be predominate with theatre-going audiences. The technique indicates that audiences will be receptive to different films at different time periods. And that these time periods—peaks and valleys—will occur at more or less regular (or irregular) intervals from three to seven years apart.

Audience desires for these changes are termed *trends*. And these trends hold for the period indicated. Each period has its own style and technique. An excellent exercise is to list all films released and the date of release. Break down the films into categories such as musicals, westerns, detective stories, comedies, horror shows, science-fiction, children's shows, love stories, action-adventure, etc. Once the categories are in order, then break down the release dates of the motion pictures. This will develop into a chart or graph and evolve into a pendulum theory. This pendulum theory chart can be projected for future filmings and choice of subject material.

ECONOMIC AND SOCIAL EFFECTS

Statistical studies have shown that during a depression in the economy, the population tends to be more conservative. They dress with duller colors and their attitudes and opinions are more restricted. They have a higher moral code, attend church more frequently and are generally more realistic.

However, their motion picture tastes lean toward more fantasies, such as love stories of the calibre of *Cinderella* and *Snow White*. During the great depression of the 1930's, America was in love with a little girl with curly blonde hair and a dimpled chin. Her father was the perpetual failure and she inevitably met the rich old banker who fell in love with her and took care of her father and herself. Audiences in those days of bleakness were able to rotate to the little girl and her father. Great stars, like Charlie Chaplin, emerged in very socially-oriented films such as *Modern Times*. The classic scene was the poor misfit working in a factory—below minimum wage, of course—tightening bolts on a never-ending assembly line.

Conversely, during a high inflationary period of economy, populations tend to be free. They dress outlandishly and colors prevail. It becomes the age of chemicals—drugs, alcohol or whatever. Church attendance goes down and the high living goes up. Motion pictures lean toward *realism* and are geared to shock the audiences. Inflationary tastes are diametrically opposed to the softer and purer fantasies of the depression era.

Motion pictures usually reflect the current mood of the country and the world. Students and motion picture distributors must be aware of all demographics. A motion picture is not necessarily successful because it is good. It is only successful when it is released at the right time. A film like *Easy Rider* would have bombed in the 1940's but because it was released in a period of high living and excitement it captured the mood and was a roaring success. It was also geared for the 18 to 30 year olds who comprised most of the audience.

In the case of westerns, a decline started in the early 1970s. However, a revival should come in the late 1970s. Projecting this analysis, it would probably be smart to think about making a western in 1979. With the decline of the westerns, the detective stories came into force. This has been very evident on television screens. They will be declining in the late 1970s.

There are some staples. In the case of the situation comedies, even these reflect the customs and the current period of sophistication. Compare the situation comedies of the late 1970s with the situation comedies of the 1950s. Social consciousness and economics have played a big part in the different dialogue and character of the newer situation comedies.

FUTURE DEMOGRAPHICS

Motion picture distributors and students must study the current markets and moods of the world population. They must project these studies into their films for future release dates. A good film takes at least one year beginning from before the start of the making of the film until completion and release date.

What are the demographics going to be in the years ahead? There are so many differentials and variables that it boggles the mind. What is the condition of the economy now and in the immediate future? What about the mood of the population? Are we at war, or will we be at war when the film is released? What party is currently in the White House, and what party will be in the White House in the immediate future? Even if a motion picture is a staple, does it reflect the current period? Will the audience accept it? These questions and many more must be asked prior to any commitment to make a motion picture.

Any producer with enough money can hire the *right* people to make a professional motion picture. Making a good film is only part of the success of the film. Making a film because one wants to is not the answer. The answer is in making a film that is geared to reflect the desires and needs of the audiences in today's market.

Everyone admires the ability of the producer to raise money and put a film together. It is a difficult and exacting job. Yet, many of these same producers are not aware of the demographics which exist. They move on instinct, and if the knowledge they have gained does not coincide with today's markets, they are totally and unequivocally out of the running. They'll have a 'bomb' and won't even be able to give the film away.

Additionally, if the student or motion picture producer makes a film which is out of the pendulum theory, it probably will not have *legs*—meaning it will not hold up. They will wonder why they are not lucky. Luck is when opportunity and preparation meet. They were not prepared.

The name of the motion picture distribution game is to make money. No company will last long in the distribution field if they continue to lose money. Unfortunately, that is the way it is. Like it or not. If any person does not realize this fact of life, he should not be in the commercial end of this business.

The basic reason for so many films lying in *film vaults* is that the producers did not take the time to study the demographics of the market. They acted compulsively, not intellectually. A specific act of intelligence is the exercise of the intellect—*to think*. If all energies were directed toward a realistic goal, every film made would be successful.

One must learn from history. Historic facts are available to every student and motion picture distributor. If one does not learn, then he must relive the same mistakes of his predecessors. However, he can have comfort in the fact that there are many failure-prone producers who refuse to open their minds and feelings.

Knowledge is power. Use it. Some day a producer may be sitting in a dark and dingy motion picture projection room watching his film. The end titles fade out on the last frame of the picture. The lights go on and everyone in the room smiles. He smiles to himself. He did his homework. He studied his market.

Chapter 2
Responsibilities Of
The Producer And Distributor

It is the responsibility of the motion picture *producer* to deliver to the motion picture *distributor* the most professional motion picture possible. The motion picture must encompass artistic as well as commercial values.

DISTRIBUTOR FUNCTIONS

It is the responsibility of the motion picture distributor to utilize all of his talents and knowledge to earn the maximum income from the distribution of the motion picture in all possible markets.

However, this income can only be obtained if the film distributor is well organized and possesses a thorough knowledge of the existing markets. He must also have the talent to exploit these markets for the motion picture producer.

This textbook is designed for students and professionals who desire to learn the functions of the motion picture film distributor. All information projected herein is the result of extensive research in the distribution field as well as personal experience in the motion picture industry. It is designed basically for the independent film maker and bridges the gap between the producer and the distributor.

FUNCTIONS OF THE PRODUCER

Once the film is completed, and prior to initial physical distribution, the producer must furnish various items to the distributor. If some of these items are not available then the distributor must obtain them and the cost of these items will be charged to the producer's account. The necessary items are:

1. A composite release print, sometimes referred to as an *answer print*, in sync sound, mounted and ready for theatre viewing. Most theatres only show 35 mm film.
2. A cut negative with action and track separate. It must correspond exactly to the composite release print referred to in item one.
3. All outtakes of prints and negative, used in the film or in the category of B negative, meaning that negative not used in the film but filmed. All sound outtakes, with corresponding coding and with editor's notes and records.
4. At least twenty-five 8 x 10 black and white or color photos depicting actual scenes occurring in the motion picture. Also, all inter-negatives of these photographs. These *stills*, as they are called, will be used for mass production for theatre displays and publicity.
5. A comprehensive cutting script used in the filming and editing of the motion picture, as well as the editor's notes and the script supervisor's notes.
6. A continuity script containing all footages as well as dialogue and music and a complete description of scenes that appear in the release print. This is vital to foreign sales and censorships as well as replacement of torn or lost film.
7. A description of the music and full music rights, footage counts as well as cue numbers for release for world-wide distribution and residual payment when applicable in both foreign and television markets.
8. A synopsis of the story line of the motion picture.
9. All press releases and suggested publicity which would be of interest to the viewing audiences, newspapers and magazines.
10. Still pictures of the cast as well as autobiographies and resumes of the artists.
11. A complete list of credits including actors, producers, directors and crew, as well as full running time of the motion picture and all other information necessary to communicate a full credit list.
12. All copies of contracts with actors, producers, directors, crews and all arrangements with any of the above both promotionally and financially.

13. A financial statement containing all accounts payable (if any), of all financial arrangements with investors and all deferments made and instructions as to payment to various individuals and companies. Also, a list of designation of payees and the order of payments, i.e., 1st, 2nd or 3rd position of payments.
14. The name and address of the re-recording studio and permission to use the full coat (magnetic tape containing separate dialogue, music and sound effects) and a description of the dubbing logs. In addition, the producer should have a 16 mm magnetic sound tape containing the music and effects only (M & E Track) for foreign sales.
15. A guarantee from the producer that he has full rights to the negative and that he has the right to make a distribution agreement.
16. All art and title work as well as textless, clear title background in 35 mm negative or inter-negative of the main and end title sections of the motion picture.
17. A letter from the producer to the film laboratory where the negatives reside giving the distributor access to all negatives on the motion picture and the right to make prints from the negatives as needed. This is called a film laboratory access letter.
18. A letter and rating from the Motion Picture Association of America with authorized Certificate of Code Rating.

Once the distributor is satisfied that he has all the proper materials required and once the producer is satisfied with the distribution fees and arrangements, then both parties are ready to sign a distribution agreement.

Chapter 3

Distribution Agreement
of the Producer and Distributor

The distribution agreement between the producer and the distributor guarantees the distributor full distribution rights. The distribution agreement usually runs for not less than three years. It can also be in perpetuity. However, the average domestic agreement is for seven years. The average foreign agreement is for five years.

The producer should ascertain the reputation and experience of the distributor prior to signing the agreement. Once the producer signs the agreement, he is virtually helpless and must rely fully on the distributor for all information about his motion picture.

The following pages illustrate a sample distribution agreement. Students and professionals should acquaint themselves with this agreement, so that if and when they are ready to sign such an agreement, they will be familiar with the contents.

The distribution agreement outlines the responsibilities of both the producer and the distributor including the terms of distribution, percentages of gross profits and the length of time the agreement will run. The distributor must have this signed agreement and letters of access to the film laboratory before he can initiate distribution functions.

DISTRIBUTION AGREEMENT

THIS AGREEMENT made and entered into as of the day of_____, by and between_____and_____, with offices in the County of Los

Angeles, State of California (hereinafter collectively referred to as the Licensor) and＿＿＿, with offices at ＿＿＿＿＿, Hollywood, California, (hereinafter referred to as the Distributor)

WITNESSETH

WHEREAS, Licensor hereby warrants that he has the exclusive right to the motion picture entitled＿＿＿＿＿, hereinafter referred to as the 'motion picture' and is desirous of granting the worldwide distribution rights hereinafter mentioned to the Distributor upon the terms and conditions hereinafter stated, and,

WHEREAS, Distributor is engaged in the business of distribution of motion pictures and is desirous of obtaining said rights hereinafter mentioned to the said motion picture, upon the terms and conditions hereinafter stated, and,

WHEREAS, the Licensor desires the Distributor to undertake distribution of the motion picture for exhibition of all forms of public and private viewing including, but not limited to theatres, private clubs, etc., throughout the world, including but without limitation, the United States and its possessions, Puerto Rico and Canada.

NOW, THEREFORE, in consideration of the mutual agreements and covenants herein contained, the parties agree as follows:

1. Rights Granted to the Distributor. The Licensor hereby grants to the Distributor, its successors, assigns and licensees, the sole and exclusive right, privilege and license, to distribute, subdistribute, license, exhibit and otherwise exploit and market throughout the world, the Picture in prints of all gauges and all forms of audio/visual display by any and all means and methods now or hereafter employed to exhibit motion pictures for theatrical and non-theatrical purposes including, without limitation, television rights, including the right to televise the Picture into theatres or other places where an admission price is charged for the right to view said telecasts. The Distributor shall have, and is hereby given and granted, full and complete discretion, except as hereinafter provided, with respect to the distribution, exhibition and other exploitation of the Picture, decisions with respect to when the Picture shall be distributed, selection of the plan or plans under which the Picture shall be distributed, exhibited and exploited and to what extent the Picture shall be withheld from distribution, exhibition or other exploitation, the selection of sub-distributors, licensees, selling agents and the manner in which the Picture is to be specifically exploited, and the extent and nature of the distribution expense to be incurred in connection with such distribution.

2. Other Rights. The Licensor agrees and covenants that it will not exercise, and will not license or authorize any other person, firm or corporation to exercise any theatrical exhibition, non-theatrical exhibition, or any other rights of any nature whatsoever with respect to the Picture for the term of the herein agreement.

18

3. Term. The term of this agreement shall commence on the date hereof and shall continue until the expiration of a period of___( ) years after delivery to the Distributor by the Licensor of the motion picture as required by paragraph 9 hereof unless terminated earlier pursuant to the terms and conditions hereof. Upon the mutual consent of the parties the term of this agreement may be extended for four (4) additional one (1) year terms, with each additional one year term requiring the approval of the parties herein.

Notwithstanding the provisions of the first sentence of this paragraph Licensor shall have the right at its sole election, to terminate or suspend this agreement pursuant to paragraph 4 hereof. Licensor's exercise of such termination or suspension rights pursuant to paragraph 4 shall not affect Licensor's obligation to pay or reimburse Distribution for its share of distribution costs pursuant to the percentages of participation stipulated in paragraph 17 below, nor the computation of payment of the Distributor's distribution fees on the net receipts derived from the distribution of the motion picture pursuant to the percentages of participation stipulated in paragraph 17.

4. Termination. Notwithstanding anything to the contrary contained in paragraph 3 hereof, Licensor shall have the right to terminate this agreement effective at the end of the first_____of the term hereof.

If Licensor elects to terminate the term of this agreement pursuant to the provisions of this paragraph 4, Distributor will, within fifteen (15) days after receipt of Licensor's written notice to such effect, advise Licensor in writing of the number of prints of the motion picture which the Distributor has in distribution or with respect to which it has actually entered into contracts for exhibiton. Licensor will reimburse the Distributor for its actual and reasonable out-of-pocket expenses incurred in connection with any print of the motion picture not yet in distribution and not yet the subject of a contract for exhibition and with respect to any expenses which the Distributor has incurred in connection with distribution arrangements that have already incurred or have occurred as the result of a contract for exhibition they shall be shared on the same basis as the percentages of participation as stipulated in paragraph 17.

5. Survival of Agreements upon Termination. Upon the termination of this agreement pursuant to any provision hereof, all rights, privileges and licenses granted to the Distributor hereby shall cease; and any agreements entered into by the Distributor with exhibitors or other sub-licensees prior to such termination shall be the sole responsibility of the Distributor following such expiration or termination.

6. Warranties. The Licensor warrants and represents as follows:

(a) That the Licensor owns and controls the exclusive right to distribute and otherwise exploit the Picture in all gauges and in any manner and form whatsoever throughout the world.

(b) That the Licensor has full right and authority to enter into and perform this agreement and represents that he has not granted to any person, firm or corporation, any of the rights in the motion picture herein granted to Distributor which might in any way impair or interfere with any of the rights herein granted to the Distributor, and Licensor agrees that he will not exercise any such rights or grant others the right to exercise any such rights.

(c) That all persons taking part or appearing in the Picture have received payment in full therefor and that there are not outstanding any obligations to pay to any person or persons any amount or amounts from, or any share or percentage of the gross or net receipts derived from any use or disposition of the Picture, or any rights herein.

(d) That synchronization rights with respect to all music and musical compositions contained in the picture are or shall be owned by the Licensor; that with respect to all music and musical compositions to be contained in the picture, the performing rights therein have been or shall be licensed by BMI, ASCAP, SESAC, or that such music is in the public domain, or that the Licensor owns or controls all the performing rights in such music for all exhibition purposes throughout the world.

(e) That no part of the Picture, or the exercise by the Distributor of any rights granted to such Licensee by the Distributor, will infringe upon or violate the common law rights or the copyright, or the literary, dramatic, musical or motion picture rights or patent rights, or the trademark or trade name, of any person; that none of the Picture violates the private, civil or property rights or the right of privacy or any other rights of any person; and that the Picture will not contain, upon delivery, any unlawful material.

(f) That the negatives of the Picture shall be of a high physical and photographic quality.

7. Indemity. The Licensor agrees to indemnify, save and hold harmless, the Distributor against, and to make good to the Distributor, any losses, damages or expense, including reasonable counsel fees and the costs of suit, incurred or suffered by the Distributor and/or its licensees, officers, directors or agents, by reason of the Licensor's violation of any agreement, warranty or representation contained in this agreement. The Licensor will bear the costs and expenses, including reasonable counsel fees, incurred by the Distributor in defending itself, its affiliates, subsidiaries and licensees who may be named as defendants in any action or proceeding in which it is claimed that the Picture infringes upon any copyright, rights of privacy, or other right of any person. In the event that any person makes any such claim, the Distributor shall have the right and power hereunder to deposit in a special bank account in a bank or trust company in the United States, such part of the Licensor's share of the Net Receipts from the Picture, as hereinafter defined, as the parties shall agree shall be sufficient to satisfy the Licensor's obligations under the indemnities herein contained. In the event that the parties hereto do not agree as to the amount to be impounded, such dispute shall be decided by arbitration before a single arbitrator selected by the American Arbitration Association and functioning pursuant to the rules and regulations of that Association. The parties consent to the jurisdiction of the Supreme Court of the State of California for purposes of enforcement of this arbitration agreement and for purposes of proceedings for the entry of judgment on any arbitration award pursuant hereto. The parties further consent that any process or notice of motion or other application to the said Supreme Court of the State of California or to a Judge thereof, may be served outside the State of California by registered mail or by personal service, provided that a reasonable time for appearance is allowed. Service in accordance herewith shall be sufficient to confer upon the said Supreme Court of the State of California jurisdiction **in personae** over the parties so served. Following the final determination of any suit or proceeding involving any such claim or after any settlement of any such claim, the Distributor shall pay over to the Licensor any portion of the Licensor's share of the net proceeds which may have been impounded as aforesaid and which is not required for payment in settlement of such suit, proceeding or claim or as an expense resulting from any breach of the Licensor's warranties hereunder shall be recouped by the Distributor from the Licensor's share of the net proceeds from the Picture. If the Distributor shall settle or compromise any suit or claim based upon any alleged state of facts which would constitute a breach by the Licensor of its warranties hereunder (and Distributor may settle and compromise any suit or claim with the consent of the Licensor, which the Licensor agrees not unreasonably to withhold) then the cost thereof shall be charges to the Licensor. Nothing contained herein shall limit the liability of the Licensor or the right of the Distributor resulting from any breach of warranty by the Licensor in the event that the Licensor's share of the net proceeds from the Picture is not sufficient to satisfy their obligations hereunder.

8. Distribution of Picture. The Distributor accepts the rights and licenses herein granted and agrees to use its best efforts, consistent with good business practices, to distribute and license the exhibition of the Picture in such manner as to obtain the largest gross receipts from the distribution and exhibition of the Picture as shall be reasonably possible.

(a) It is understood that all expenses involved in screenings, the need for additional 35 mm and/or 16 mm prints, cost of shipping positive prints and/or negatives, storage charges, etc., in connection with screening prints to effect sales will be shared on the same basis as the percentages of participation as stipulated in paragraph 17 hereof.

9. Delivery. Delivery, at any place or places mutually acceptable to the Licensor and the Distributor, shall consist of:

(a) One first class complete 35 mm original and/or dupe negative, and transferred optical sound track and_____35 mm composite prints thereof. Licensor hereby also agrees that if, in Distributor's opinion it is necessary to make shipment of a dupe negative to a foreign country, Distributor shall have the right to do so, provided that the negative, properly insured, will remain in said foreign country in bond, and be used for the striking off of the required number of positive prints and be immediately thereafter returned to the laboratory in the United States. All costs incurred in connection with the shipping of the dupe negative to a foreign country shall be shared on the same basis as the percentages of participation as stipulated in paragraph 17 herein.

(b) No less than twenty-five (25) still photographs, being both production stills and specially posed stills of principals.

(c) One copy of each final shooting script.

(d) Pressbooks, minimum

(e) One sheet, minimum

(f) Trailers, minimum

(g) Distributor understands that accessories are handled by National Screen Service Corporation and Distributor agrees to notify all exhibitors to obtain accessories from said or such other company as shall be designated by the Licensor.

10. Inspection of Agreements. Upon demand by the Distributor, the Licensor will submit for inspection by the Distributor's attorneys or other authorized representatives, the following, with respect to the Picture:

(a) All sound royalty agreements, employment agreements with the principal actors, the director and the producer, and a certificate to the effect that all costs, expenses or charges incurred in connection with the production of each picture, except deferments or trade credits, arranged in accordance with the provision of this agreement or expressly authorized or approved in writing by the Distributor or fully subordinated to the rights of the Distributor hereunder, have been paid in full.

(b) All licenses, contracts, assignments and/or other written permissions from the proper parties in interest permitting the Licensor or its predecessor or predecessors in interest to use any musical, literary, dramatic and other material of whatever nature used in the production of the Picture.

11. Title to Picture and Reserved Rights. The Licensor shall own and retain the title to the Picture and to all negatives, duplicate negatives and prints thereof. Upon the termination thereof, negatives, duplicate negatives and prints thereof. Upon the termination thereof, the Distributor will deliver to the Licensor, or their nominee,

all positive prints of the picture then in its possession. All rights in, or in connection with the Picture and/or with all literary, dramatic, musical and other material contained therein, which are not expressly granted or licensed hereunder to the Distributor, are reserved to the Licensor.

12. Credits. The Distributor shall not alter or remove from the

Picture any credits to persons performing services in or contributing any material of any nature to the production thereof, with out the written consent of the Licensor. The Distributor may add to the Picture appropriate credits or insignia, or both, to the effect that the Picture is distributed by and through the Distributor.

13. Liens. Neither of the parties hereto will hypothecate, encumber or allow any lien to be created against the negative, dupe negatives or any sound track of the Picture without the prior written consent of both parties hereto.

14. Editing. The Distributor shall have the right subject to the written consent of the Licensor, to the extent necessary to meet requirements imposed by local, federal, or international regulations, to edit the picture, including additional scenes, retakes and/or cuts. The cost of such changes shall be shared on the same basis as the percentages of participation as stipulated in paragraph 17 herein. All other changes shall be subject to the Licensor's prior written approval and, when so approved the expenses shall be similarly shared as above.

15. Distribution Practices. In entering into agreements for exhibition of the Picture, the Distributor shall observe the following:

(a) The Distributor shall not be entitled to any compensation with respect to any film rentals or license fees which shall not be paid by exhibitor, it being agreed that the Distributor shall be entitled to its said share only with respect to net film rentals paid by exhibitors to the Distributor or to its Trustee.

16. Receipts. As used herein, the term 'Gross Receipts' from the picture shall mean and include all sums and amounts received by or on behalf of the Distributor from or on account of the lease, license, exhibition, distribution, sub-distribution, marketing, turning account, or other disposition of the Picture, or any rights therein pursuant hereto, whether such receipts are received during the term hereof or after the expiration thereof. 'Gross Receipts' shall not be deemed to include any monies derived from the Picture in the currency of foreign countries. Monies derived from the exploitation of the Picture in foreign countries shall be included in Gross Receipts only after the same have been converted, as permitted by local foreign law, into United States Dollars and transmitted to the Licensor or the Distributor, as the case maybe, in Los Angeles, California. The net amount remitted after deducting the costs and expenses involved in converting said foreign currency and transmitting the same shall be included in Gross Receipts to be accounted for hereunder. As used herein, the term 'Net Receipts' for the Picture shall mean the amounts remaining after the deduction of the following:

(a) The aggregate actual cost and expenses incurred by the Distributor and the Licensor for prints of the Picture and other laboratory charges.

(b) The amounts of any standard advertising agency commissions paid by the Distributor upon prior written approval of the Licensor.

(c) All sums expended or incurred by the Distributor for advertising purposes upon prior written approval of the Licensor.

(d) The amounts required to be paid under the provisions of any collective bargaining agreement with any union or guild on account of any 'reuse' or 'rerun' of the Picture. The Licensor agrees to promptly advise Distributor of all obligations under union or guild contracts to make any such payments.

(e) All amounts required to be paid by or on behalf of the Distributor as state, county, city or other taxes based upon the value of the Picture and all sums required to be paid by the Distributor as imposts, taxes and like charges assessed or levied by any duly constituted taxing authority, based upon or relating to the gross monies derived on account of or from the distribution or exhibition of the Picture, whether such taxes are denominated as turn-over taxes, sales taxes, remittance taxes, film hire taxes, gross business taxes, or by any other denomination. Nothing herein contained shall permit the deduction from Gross Receipts of any income, franchise, excess profits or similar tax upon the Distributor or its licensees.

(f) All advances by Distributor to defray cost of furnishing dialogue continuities of the Picture when requested by the Distributor for dubbing purposes.

(h) The costs of import fees and licenses and other similar requirements to secure the right to import and distribute the Picture into or out of any foreign country.

(i) All taxes, duties, imposts and like charges assessed or levied by any taxing authority for which the Distributor may be held liable, computed, levied or assessed upon the Licensor's share and any and all legal expenses; including reasonable attorney's fees, incurred by the Distributor in contesting the imposition of any tax deductible under this subparagraph.

(j) All expenses incurred by the Distributor in copyrighting the Picture in the name of the Licensor upon the prior written approval of the Licensor.

(k) The cost and expense incurred in connection with employing checkers, in the case of percentage engagements, generally known as house checking expenses.

(l) Any other deduction from film rental expressly authorized in a written exhibition agreement with any exhibitor,

(m) In the event any film is confiscated by any legal authority, Distributor is authorized to expend up to $1,000 in order to obtain possession of the confiscated film and defend any legal action brought against the exhibitor, Distributor or Producer. Any expenditures that exceed $1,000 in connection with obtaining possession of such film that has been confiscated or defending such legal action shall be approved by the Licensor in writing before the same is made.

(n) All monies expended for the following upon prior written approval of the Licensor.

1. Art work
2. Press books
3. Still photos
4. Posters (one sheets)
5. Release prints
6. Trailers
7. Editing
8. Equipment rentals
9. Shipping cases and reel
10. Permafilming
11. Film repair

The amounts remaining from the Net Receipts after deduction of the items enumerated from (a) to (n) in this paragraph shall be paid over to the Distributor as distribution fees pursuant to paragraph 17 and the remainder of the Net Receipts after the payment of the distribution fees shall be paid to the Licensor as its portion of the Net Receipts.

17. Distribution Fees. Distribution fees shall be the following percentage of the Net Receipts:

(a) From any National Exhibition of the Picture,_____Percent ( ) National Exhibition means exhibition of any motion picture in the United States and or its possessions or mandates.

(b) From any Foreign Exhibition of the Picture,_____Percent ( ). Foreign Exhibition means exhibition of the Picture outside the Continental United States.

(c) From all other sources,_____Percent ( ).

18. Records to be Maintained by Distributor. The Distributor shall maintain complete, true and accurate books and records which shall reflect, in accordance with approved bookkeeping practices, all Gross Receipts realized, as hereinbefore defined and also reflecting all costs and expenses which the Distributor is permitted to deduct from Gross Receipts under the terms of this agreement. Such books and records shall be open for inspection by the Licensor or its representatives, during reasonable business hours upon demand. The Licensor or its representatives shall be permitted to make copies or excerpts thereof and of all licenses and other instruments relating to any permitted exhibition or use of the Picture.

19. Accounting by Distributor. The Distributor shall furnish to the licensor on a_____basis a statement as to receipts received at its home office during the preceding week from exhibitors of the motion picture and quarterly statements setting forth the Gross Receipts from the Picture and detailed statements of the deductions therefrom all as provided herein. Each such quarterly statement shall be delivered no later than ten (10) days after the close of each such quarterly period. The Licensor shall have thirty (30) days from the date of delivery of each such statement within which to deliver to the Distributor any and all written objections; objections not raised during such thirty (30) day period shall be forever foreclosed and the statements shall thereupon be deemed true, accurate, final and binding upon the parties and all other persons.

20. Remittance by Distributor. Subject to the provisions hereof, the Distributor shall remit to the Licensor the sums shown to be due to them on each quarterly statement, and such remittance shall accompany such statements.

21. Frozen Funds. If, by reason of a moratorium, embargo or banking or other restriction, the Distributor finds it impracticable or impossible to have any monies derived from the Picture in foreign countries transmitted to Los Angeles, California, it shall be under no obligation to pay the Licensor's share, if any, of such monies until such moratorium, embargo, banking or other restriction is lifted and the monies are actually received by the Distributor in Los Angeles, California. The Distributor shall have the right to deal with and treat such frozen monies in the same manner in which it deals with and treats generally other frozen funds, and provided that the Distributor shall have dealt or does so deal with the Licensor's funds in a reasonable manner; the Distributor's judgment wih respect thereto shall be conclusive and binding upon the Licensor. It is further agreed that the Distributor will exercise reasonable effort to procure the transmission to the United States of the Licensor's share of such monies as promptly as reasonably possible at the prevailing rate of exchange and that if the Distributor is able to secure transmission of the Licensor's share of such monies, or any part thereof, to Los Angeles, the parties hereto will bear the equal cost and expense involved in any such transmission unless the Licensor does not agree to be bound by the terms, provisions and conditions of any agreements heretofore or hereafter made by the Distributor with other American distributors of motion pictures, or with any Government relating to remittance from any country or territory to the United States. The Distributor shall not deduct from funds in the United States the distribution fees to which it would otherwise be entitled from collections with respect to the Picture which are frozen or are otherwise restricted, but all distribution fees shall be payable and deducted only in the currency in which earned. If the transmission of monies from any foreign territory or country to the United States is prevented by embargo, moratorium or other restriction, then if the Licensor shall so request in writing within sixty (60) days from the date when the Licensor is first notified in writing by the Distributor that the transmission of such monies is thus prevented by embargo, moratorium or other restriction, and if permitted by the laws of such territory or country, the Distributor shall deposit the share of the net proceeds to which the Licensor would be entitled upon transmission to Los Angeles, in the Licensor's name in any bank or other depository designated by the Licensor in such territory or country. Such deposit shall, for the purpose hereof, be deemed payment to the Licensor of the amount so deposited (computed at the official rate of exchange) and the Distributor shall have no further liability of any kind or nature in connection with sums so deposited.

22. Breach and Termination. In the event that either party breaches any of the terms, conditions, covenants or restrictions set forth herein and fails to cure, correct and remedy the same within thirty (30) days after receipt of written notice to the party so in default then, at the election of the party not in default this agreement shall terminate and all licenses granted hereunder shall likewise terminate, except as provided herein.

23. Force Majeure. Neither party hereto shall be liable to the other in damages or otherwise because of failure or delay in performance caused by war (whether or not there has been any official declaration thereof) strike, lockout, labor controversy, inability to obtain materials, transportation, labor, power, or other essential commodity, fire, flood, epidemic, earthquake, explosion, casualty, riot, civil disturbance, act of a public enemy, embargo, *force majeure*, any governmental, executive or administrative decree or rule or regulation, or any other cause beyond its control.

24. Copyright. The Distributor shall have the right to make, in the name of the Licensor, registration of a claim to copyright in the United States Copyright Office on the Picture as to which claim to copyright was not theretofore made by the Licensor. The Licensor shall execute any and all papers required for the Distributor to effect such registration. The costs of effecting such registration may be deducted by the Distributor from the Gross Receipts as hereinbefore defined.

25. Junking of Prints. In the event that, during the term of this agreement, any of the prints of the Picture in the possession of the Distributor are, in its judgment, no longer in usable condition, the Distributor upon prior written approval of the Licensor may dispose of them and furnish to the Licensor an affidavit stating the facts of such disposition. If at any time during such term the Distributor, in its reasonable judgment, determines that the number of prints in its possession is excessive, the Distributor may notify the Licensor in writing of such determination, specifying the number of such excess prints and giving the Licensor an option to request either (a) the shipment of such excess prints to the Licensor at the Licensor's expense, or (b) the junking of such prints. In the event that the Licensor fails to notify the Distributor in writing within thirty (30) days after receipt of such notice that it has selected either of these alternatives, the Distributor shall be authorized to junk such excess prints. Any income resulting from the junking of excess prints hereunder shall inure to the benefit of the Licensor exclusively.

26. Advertising and Publicity. The Distributor and its licensees, except as herein provided as to the necessities of prior written approval are granted the exclusive right to publicize and advertise the Picture throughout the world during the term hereof, and to cause or permit others to do so. The Distributor is granted complete discretion except as herein provided in paragraph 16 as to the manner and method of advertising and publicizing the Picture. In the promotion of the Picture, the Distributor undertakes to comply with Licensor's commitments in regard to the credits to be granted any person provided that Distributor is notified of such commitments and provided further that such commitments are customarily incurred by producers of motion picture films. The Distributor and its licensees may, in promoting the Picture, disseminate, reproduce, print and publish the names, biographies and likenesses of the principal members of the cast, the writer, the producer and the director connected with the production of the picture provided that this does not extend to any endorsement of any product. For the promotion of the pictures, Licensor agrees to furnish one trailer to Distributor and from time to time as may be needed additional trailers when so requested by Distributor. The cost of any additional trailers shall be shared on the same basis as the percentage of participation as stipulated in paragraph 17.

27. Action Against Third Persons. If any person shall do or perform any act or acts which the Distributor believes constitutes a copyright infringement with respect to the Picture or any of the literary, dramatic or musical material contained in the Picture, or constitutes a plagiarism or violates or infringes any right of the Licensor or of the Distributor therein, or if any person shall do or perform any act or acts which the Distributor believes constitutes an unauthorized or unlawful distribution, exhibition or use of the Picture, then and in any such event, the Distributor may and shall have the right to take such steps and to institute such suits or proceedings as the Distributor may deem advisable or necessary to prevent such acts and conduct and to obtain damages and other relief and generally to take such steps as may be necessary or proper, in the judgment of the Distributor, for the full protection of the rights of the parties. The Distributor may take such steps or institute such suits or proceedings in its own name or in the name of the Licensor or in the names of the parties hereto jointly, and the Distributor is hereby appointed and constituted the lawful attorney-in-fact of the Licensor to do all acts and things permitted or contemplated by the terms of this paragraph. The Distributor shall be entitled to recoup from the Gross Receipts of the Picture its reasonable costs and expenses (including reasonable attorney's fees) paid or incurred in connection with the foregoing; provided, however, that if any collections are effected by compromise or judgement, such expenses shall first be deducted from such collections. The remainder of such collections, if any, shall be deemed part of the Gross Receipts from the Picture. Nothing herein contained shall be deemed a limitation or restriction of the indemnity provisions set forth in paragraph 7 hereof.

28. Relationship of the Parties. Nothing herein contained shall be interpreted or construed or is intended by the parties hereto to constitute a partnership or joint venture between the parties hereto, or be construed to make either party hereto the agent of the other party. Each of the parties agrees that it will not hold itself out as the agent of the other party by advertising or otherwise and neither of the parties shall be or become liable or bound by any representation, act, omission or agreement whatsoever of the other party hereto, it being the intent and agreement of the parties hereto that neither shall enter into any agreement or commitment binding upon or obligating the other to any extent. For purposes of this paragraph and of this agreement generally, the Licensor constitutes_____, and_____, and the Distributor constitutes_____.

29. Definition of "Person". Except where the context shall otherwise require, the term "person," as used herein, includes any association, organization, partnership, business trust or corporations, as well as natural persons.

30. Controlling Law. This agreement shall be interpreted in accordance with the laws of the State of California.

31. Assignments. This agreement shall not be assignable by the Distributor without the prior written consent of the Licensor.

Notwithstanding, the Licensor shall at all times during the term of this agreement have the right to assign its interest in the Gross Receipts to be collected herein.

32. Insurance. The obligation hereunder to obtain or to keep in force and effect any insurance with respect to any composite print or the negative of the motion picture shall be the sole responsibility of the _____.

33. Notices. All notices, payments, accountings or other data which the Distributor is required or may desire to send or deliver to the Licensor shall either be delivered in person to an officer of the Licensor, or shall be mailed in the United States mails, postage prepaid, to the Licensor at _____ or to such other address as the Licensor may designate, from time to time, in writing. All notices, payments, accountings and other data which the Licensor is required or may desire to send or deliver to the Distributor herein shall either be delivered in person to an officer of the Distributor, or shall be mailed in the United States mails, postage prepaid, to the Distributor at _____ or to such other address as the Distributor may designate, from time to time, in writing. Notices hereunder may also be sent by telegraph, toll prepaid, addressed to the aforesaid address of a party. Delivery shall conclusively be deemed to have occurred on the day following mailing or delivery to a telegraph company as herein provided.

34. Dubbing. The_____shall determine whether it wishes to have any dubbed versions of the Picture and in what language said dubbed versions are to be made. Licensor shall thereupon furnish as promptly as practicable the Distributor with such completed dubbed versions ready for printing; or in the alternative, the Licensor may direct the Distributor to arrange for the preparation of dubbed versions. In either event the Licensor shall bear the entire cost of such dubbed versions, and if the Distributor advances the cost of dubbing, the Licensor authorizes the Distributor to recoup the amount of such advances from the Gross Receipts as defined in paragraph 16.

35. Entire Agreement. This agreement expresses the entire understanding of the parties hereto and replaces any and all former agreements, understandings, or representations relating in any way to the subject matter hereof.

36. Binding. This agreement shall inure to and be binding upon the Licensor and the Distributor, their heirs, executors, administrators and assigns.

37. Change in Writing. This agreement may not be changed or supplemented except in writing signed by both parties hereto.

IN WITNESS WHEREOF, the parties hereto have caused this agreement to be executed the day and year first above written.

(PRODUCER)

BY _____

(DISTRIBUTOR)

BY _____

Chapter 4
Publicity Campaign

The layman knows the term *coming attractions*. However, in the distribution industry *coming attractions* are called *trailers*.

Motion Picture Trailers, Television Trailers and Radio Spots are probably the most important sales tool to the viewing audiences. The theatre and television audiences are bombarded with these visuals long before they see the motion picture.

A trailer is nothing more than a very fast synopsis of the motion picture. Since it does not follow any form of continuity, many optical tricks can be used to show the audience what is in the picture and yet not tell the entire storyline.

MOTION PICTURE TRAILERS

Motion Picture trailers usually run between two and three minutes and normally show the best parts of the motion picture. They are basically teasers designed to get the audience into the theatres. They must be visually exciting and when the trailer ends the people should want to see the film.

Trailers use music and dialogue to sell the audiences. They implant desires and anticipation. However, they must still leave an unfulfilled feeling. This feeling can only be fulfilled by seeing the entire film.

In order for the distributor to edit and create the trailer, he must have all film available as outlined in chapter 2 under items two and three. To obtain this film, the distributor submits to the

PRODUCER'S LETTERHEAD

DATE_____

Name and address of film laboratory

Re: "Name of film and production number"

Gentlemen:

This will advise you that our firm (name of production company), (hereinafter called the "Licensor," has granted, pursuant to a distribution agreement of even date, to (name and address of distribution company) (hereinafter called the "Licensee"), the exclusive sales and distribution rights for a period of____years from even date, for the motion picture entitled (name of film) for all world markets.

We hereby represent and warrant that there is on deposit in your laboratory negative of such condition as to permit the manufacture therefrom of commercially acceptable release prints in 35 mm and 16 mm gauge, and for the manufacturer of additional cut negative which can be commercially acceptable to use as a motion picture trailer.

We, hereby, authorize, direct and instruct you, and you agree, to fill all orders from Licensee at Licensee's cost and expense, for positive prints of, or other laboratory services and materials (including inter-positives and inter-negatives) with respect to the picture, as Licensee from time to time may order, subject to Licensee's ability to meet its obligations at your laboratory. You agree to deliver to Licensee, upon their request, such material as they may order.

You agree, however, that you shall not permit the original negatives of the picture to be removed from your possession during the term of the Distribution Agreement without the written consent of the undersigned and the Licensee. We also agree not to order preprints of the negatives or remove the negative from your film laboratory without the written consent of the Licensee.

All materials which you may supply to or on order of Licensee are to be paid for solely by Licensee. You agree that Licensor shall not be liable to pay any of your charges which may be

Fig. 4-1. A sample film access letter.

incurred by Licensee for any services or material relating to the picture, and that you will neither refuse to process Licensor's orders for material and services relating to the picture nor assert any lien on the picture or any material relating thereto as against Licensor by reason of the failure of Licensee to pay charges which they may incur for materials or services relating to the picture.

You agree that Licensee shall not be liable to pay any of your charges which may be incurred by Licensor or any of Licensor's Licensees for any service and materials relating to the picture and that you will neither refuse to process Licensee's orders for materials and services relating to the picture nor assert any lien to the picture or any materials relating thereto as against Licensee by reason of the failure of Licensor or any of Licensor's Licensees to pay any charges which they may incur for services and materials relating to the picture, except that your laboratory shall comply with all applicable federal, state and local statutes.

We agree that we will not assign any additional access film agreements with any other company or individual while this access letter is in force. Please indicate your agreement to the foregoing by signing in the space provided below.

Very truly yours,

(PRODUCER'S COMPANY)

By ——————————
(authorized signature)

AGREED TO AND ACCEPTED:_____

DATE:_____

(NAME OF FILM LABORATORY)

By_____

(authorized signature)

laboratory the *film access letter* mentioned previously. The letter is written on the producer's stationery (Fig. 4-1). The Distributor initates many more actions. He orders from the film laboratory certain pieces of the cut negative by making a CRI (color reversal inter-negative) and by using the outtakes (B negative not used in the finished film).

He also orders from the sound re-recording studio certain pieces of sound including dialogue, music and effects. From this the distributor is able to use same as a work print to cut action. The film is called *action* and the sound is called *track*.

These two items, together with dialogue, music and sound, are all that will be necessary to edit an exciting trailer. Once all the scenes are cut, it is necessary to do *voice over dialogue* on the trailer. This is accomplished by means of another re-recording session in which all the elements are mixed. The dialogue track is separate on the full coat—the magnetic tape—and the balance of music and effects are used for foreign sales. Each country can then insert their own dialogue track and then all elements will be in sync.

TELEVISION TRAILERS

From the material contained in the cut trail·r, the distributor also makes a one minute spot TV trailer; a 20 second spot TV trailer and a 10 second spot TV trailer. This is accomplished by making CRI's of the cut 35 mm film and re-recording these spots. After this has been accomplished, the Distributor makes a reduction 16 mm film and a 35/32 track. This track is spliced down the middle for two 16 mm sound prints.

RADIO SPOTS

The sound portions of the trailer are used for radio spots of 10 and 20 second durations.

All TV trailers and Radio Spots will be used later for publicity and advertising when the film is ready to be played in theatres.

CRI PRINTS

All film laboratories print from a CRI instead of the original negative. The reason for this is that if the CRI tears in the re-printing, then the laboratory can make another CRI of the torn section and splice the new section into the original CRI. Also, in the case of foreign sales, many times the foreign buyer borrows the

CRI to strike prints in his own country. This way, he can use local currencies and, in addition, he does not pay import duties. Once the CRI is made, then the laboratory will be ready for the mass printing of the motion picture. In the case of the cut trailers, the distributor orders a new CRI of the trailer for mass printings. The distributor orders a *textless version* of the trailer for foreign countries.

All of the above will be accomplished as soon as the distributor receives the motion picture code rating referred to in Chapter 5.

PRESSBOOKS

From the motion picture stills (8 x 10s) mentioned in Chapter 2 under item 4, and all other advertising materials mentioned under items 8, 9, 10 and 16 of Chapter 2, the distributor starts work on the *pressbooks and one sheets*.

The pressbooks and the one sheets are probably the most important sales tools a distributor can have, since the exhibitor (theatre owner) books the motion picture from his reactions to the pressbook. Many times exhibitors do not even see the motion picture and this makes the pressbook doubly important as a sales tool.

The pressbook contains all key art of the film which is used in all campaigns including newspaper ads, synopsis, full credits of crew and cast, running time and various publicity ideas and promotional material. The motion picture stills show the leading artists and include a brief resume of their background for newspaper blurbs. The pressbook sets up the entire publicity campaign and initiates the key art and logos. It is the pivot for all promotion of the film.

There are many different forms and sizes of pressbooks. However, the motion picture industry concentrates on a standard size. The standard size pressbook runs 11-1/2 inches wide and 9 inches long when folded and fits into a standard envelope of 9 x 12. The pressbook is designed so that it can fold into four to six pages depending on the number of pages desired. However, the length will always remain 18 inches long.

A sample six page pressbook is broken down as follows:

First Page. This is the key art of the motion picture and this page blown up is also used as the one sheets (Fig. 4-2).

Second Page. This page contains the synopsis of the story, the cast list, the crew credit list as well as resumes and pictures of the artists (Fig. 4-3).

Third Page. This page concerns the advertising ads with various sizes of ads. These ads can be cut out of the pressbook by theatres and submitted to the newspapers for re-printing (Fig. 4-4). See chapter 11.

Page Four. The fourth page of a pressbook also contains advertising ads and has various sizes for newspapers (Fig. 4-5).

Page Five. Page five deals with the publicity and sales promotion

Fig. 4-2. Key art of the motion picture. This page is also used as a one sheet. (Photo courtesy of Films International).

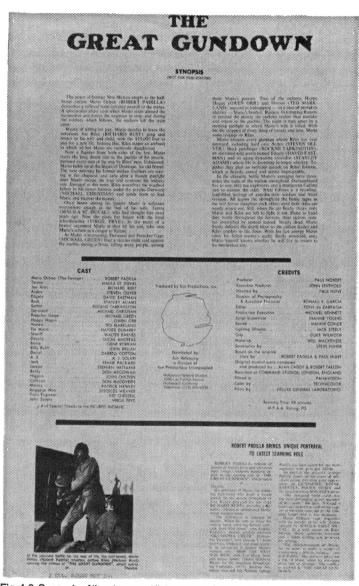

Fig. 4-3. Synopsis of the story, cast list, crew credit, list, pictures of artists. (Photo courtesy of Films International).

of the motion picture. It is the full publicity campaign designed for theatre and magazine promotional stories about the artists (Fig. 4-6).

Page Six. This page shows the one sheets available. They can be in various sizes but the standard size is 27 x 41. Page six also informs the theatre owner that lobby stills (8 x 10s) are available in sets of 25. This page also informs the theatre where accessories and trailers are available (Fig. 4-7). See chapter 10.

When printing, the pressbook is printed in color for pages one, five and six (back sheet); and in black and white for pages two,

Fig. 4-4. Various sizes of ads. (Photo courtesy of Films International).

three and four (inside sheet). After printing the sheets are folded into three folds.

ONE SHEETS

One sheets are made from the first page of the pressbook. This art work is copied to a new negative and is blown up to a 27 x

Fig. 4-5. Ad sizes available for newspapers. (Photo courtesy of Films International).

41 inch poster. These posters are used outside the theatre usually in glass frames. One sheets are extremely important, in that, at times, the theatre audience is attracted into the theatre by the one sheet alone.

Fig. 4-6. Publicity designed for theatre and magazine promotional stories about the artists. (Photo courtesy of Films international).

Fig. 4-7. Illustration of one sheets available. (Photo courtesy of Films International).

The distributor must use his vast experience and knowledge in making the pressbooks. All costs of the pressbooks and one sheets are charged to the producer's account and he must pay for them out of his share of the profits of the motion picture.

Chapter 5
Motion Picture Code Rating

After the signing of the distribution agreement, the distributor has many duties and functions to perform.

Item 18 of Chapter 2 refers to a letter and rating from the Motion Picture Association of America with an authorized Certificate of Code Rating. In most cases, the motion picture producer does not get this rating for him.

Since all advertising materials as well as trailers (coming attractions) must have the code rating (Table 5-1), the distributor usually wants the rating prior to any necessary work being done on the film, the pressbook, the trailer and the one sheets. These items were explored in Chapter 4.

The cost of the code rating is for the account of the producer. The distributor may advance coding costs and recoup same from the producer's share of income. While the distributor is arranging for the rating code, his office will also be doing other functions.

MOTION PICTURE ASSOCIATION OF AMERICA

However, the MPAA code ratings are so important that a study of the organization, its rules and regulations, and its position in the motion picture industry is worth devoting the entire contents of this chapter.

The history of the Motion Picture Association of America and its rules and regulations are explored in depth in Table 5-2. The student and professional will be aware of the power of the

Table 5-1. Advertising Materials and the MPAA Rating.

HOW TO WORK MOST EFFECTIVELY WITH THE ADVERTISING DEPARTMENT OF THE CODE AND RATING ADMINISTRATION

The main function of the Advertising Department is to review advertising material in advance so that the motion picture distributor will meet fewer problems in having his material accepted by the several media channels—newspaper, television, radio and theatre audiences. Though we cannot guarantee that MPAA approved material will be accepted by every newspaper, television or radio station, we do know that it will be acceptable to practically all of them. In fact we will follow up for you with the media (as we have done many times in the past), if you run into difficulties with approved ads.

The following paragraphs are a few guidelines that will be helpful to both you and the MPAA concerning the submission of advertising material.

THE MPAA RATING MUST BE USED IN ALL ADVERTISING.

II. PRINT ADVERTISING

This includes everthing but theatre trailers and radio and TV spots.

A. STILLS

First, submit your proposed advertising and publicity stills in advance for approval. In this way you will avoid making up a complete series of advertisements of unapproved material that may require redoing a whole campaign after it has been plated. It is much more costly to revise metal than to make a minor deletion or revision in a still.

B. NEWSPAPER ADS

Submit the theme of the campaign on paper and any ad headlines that you think might be questionable to the MPAA. The earlier you get the okay the better. You can then go to finish with confidence and the assurance that your final print material will be approved without question.

C. POSTERS

Submit art work and layouts for posters well in advance, even before the final rating of the picture. You can always add the correct rating symbol later. Use of rating symbol and full definition required on all posters.

D. PRESSBOOKS

Never go to a final pressbook print unless all of the advertising elements and publicity stills used have been given earlier MPAA approval.

Once every thing in your pressbook is submitted and approved please add the following notice for all films rated either "G," "PG," or "R" (not "X") in a prominent place:

APPROVED

All advertising in this pressbook, as well as all other advertising and publicity materials referred to herein, has been approved under the standards for Advertising of the Code of Self-Regulation of the Motion Picture Association of America. All inquiries on this procedure may be addressed to:

Director of the Code of Advertising Motion Picture Association of America

This picture was rated:

Please fill in official MPAA rating and definition (slug) that applies to your film.

organization and the help it furnishes to the entire motion picture industry. There are two things which are very important to motion picture distributors, producers and students:

■ A motion picture film library which has 9000 books, pamphlets and periodicals about the motion picture industry; 50,000 still photographs; and files on approximately 40,000 films dating back to 1894.

■ A motion picture code which gives official MPAA ratings on films.

The Motion Picture Association of America furnishes the above. They also furnish *Oscars* to winners of best films. The Academy of Motion Picture Arts and Sciences celebrated its 50th anniversary in 1977. Since its inception it has been a strong driving force in the motion picture industry. Their publication of *The Players Directory* is a service producers have been using since 1937. The Players Directory is published three times a year listing over 8500 performing actors and their agents. It is the *casting bible* and only bonafide artists can be listed.

RATING CERTIFICATIONS

The primary function of the MPAA insofar as motion picture distributors are concerned is to give necessary ratings to their motion pictures. Without these ratings most newspapers in the United States as well as theatres will not play the film. This is also the case with television stations and radio stations. The first thing a motion picture distributor asks a producer is 'Did you get a rating yet?' The producer retorts, 'I thought you'd get it for me.' After all, you don't need a rating to show the film to a distributor but the distributor needs the rating to exhibit and sell the film.

Table 5-2. MPAA Rules and Regulations.

THEATRE TRAILERS

The theatre trailer is the key element in every motion picture distribution campaign. We are aware of the importance of the theatre trailer to every distributor and exhibitor. We also know—all too well—that it is one of the most sensitive areas in the industry's film rating program. Use of the official MPAA rating tag is required to be shown on all trailers for rated films. There are no audio requirements for theatrical trailers.

A trailer for General Audiences (green-banded) and television spots have the same standards. Often times the 60-second television spot is used as a "teaser" or "cross-plug" trailer for General Audiences.

No blood can be shown in either a television spot or a General Audience (green-banded) trailers.

The trailer tag reflects the rating of The feature.

G—Unrestricted Audience

A family audience enjoying a "G"-rated film may object to a trailer they may feel is unsuitable for their children who may be with them. Parents can be very protective about what they didn't select, and resent material that may be thrust upon them because they happen to be in the audience. We have brought the trailer situation under control and it is important to retain public confidence.

We examine trailers and approve them for two audiences— "G" Unrestricted Audiences—and "R" Restricted (Under 17 must be accompanied by parent or adult guardian). All trailers for "PG" films must be suitable for "G" audiences, regardless of the content of the "PG" film. Remember, a patron selects a "PG" film after having been warned concerning the content. This does not mean that all of the material in the film can play to a "G" Unrestricted Audience.

It is important to keep this fact in mind when preparing trailers—and this applies particularly to indepedents who may be working on their first feature release.

A trailer for General Audiences (green-banded) and television spots have the same standards. Often times the 60-second televison spot is used as a "teaser" or "cross-plug" trailer for General Audiences.

No blood can be shown in either a television spot or a General Audience (green-banded) trailer.

R—Restricted Audience

In the case of "R"-rated films, frequently a distributor requests that we review his trailer so that it will be acceptable to play with Unrestricted Audiences, and carry a green band. (National Screen Service uses a green shipping band on Unrestricted Audience trailers, and a red band on Restricted Audience trailers.)

If a trailer for an R or X feature approved for General Audiences does not carry the special "R" tag for General Audiences, many exhibitors will not play the trailer.

Table 5-2. MPAA Rules and Regulations (continued from page 45).

The Advertising Code Dept. must then request that all scenes unsuitable for a "G" audience—the most sensitive area in the Unrestricted Audience—be deleted.

It should be clearly understood that "Red Banded" trailers for R and X audiences cannot carry the same scenes of sex and violence that may be approved in the R rated feature. The advertising must necessarily eliminate all strong sex or excessive violence in theatre trailers.

We suggest you use the following procedures. Let us look at your rough cut before going to a composite. And even before we see it, you should eliminate excessive violence—close-up shooting, stabbings, hacking with axes, etc. Show the weapon, not the meeting against flesh. Eliminate all blood possible. If guns are fired, do not use close-up shots where the bullet hits a body, but cut to body on the ground or just before body hits the ground. Avoid bloody scenes or close-up of blood on dead bodies. This material just does not play to the families in "G" audiences.

No exposed breasts or bed scenes with any action will be approved. Even if partners are fully clothed, sexually oriented material will not be acceptable in "G" auidence trailers.

Where making a "G" audience trailer is not possible with an "R"-rated feature, we suggest accepting a Red Banded Restricted Audience trailer and using a one-minute TV spot for the "G"-Unrestricted Audience trailer. Many companies do this successfully.

TELEVISION SPOTS

All television trailers should be made with an Unrestricted Audience in mind. Rough material such as sexual references, excessive violence, blood, or strong language, is not acceptable in TV spots. The Association will request deletions when the material seems to be out of line for TV—but otherwise we will warn the advertiser that the spot may be held up for telecasting until after 9:00 P.M. or even after 11:00 P.M. before it will be approved by a TV station for use.

The MPAA Advertising Regulations which follow, give specific information on the use of the rating symbol in TV spots both visually and verbally in 60-30-20 and 10-second spots. This arrangement was worked out in cooperation with the National Association of Broadcasters and must be carefully adhered to.

TV spots should carry rating and definition large enough to be legible on a home viewer's screen (four seconds). Can be on same frame with film title and credits.

NOTE: IN PAST EXPERIENCES WHEN THE STATIONS FELT THAT THE RATING AND DEFINITION WERE NOT LARGE ENOUGH, THEY WOULD FLASH ON AN ADDITIONAL COPY OF THE RATING AND DEFINITION, USUALLY IN LARGE WHITE LETTERS, OVER SCENES IN THE SPOT.

REGULATIONS FOR TV SPOTS
60-30-20-10 Second Spots
VISUAL Show the MPAA Seal

Table 5-2. MPAA Rules and Regulations (continued from page 46).

Show the Rating Symbol Letter—(G, PG, R, X)
Show the Full Definition of the Symbol

Full Definition:

G—GENERAL AUDIENCES
All Ages Admitted

PG—PARENTAL GUIDANCE SUGGESTED
Some Material may not be Suitable for Pre-Teenagers

R—RESTRICTED
Under 17 Requires Accompanying Parent or Adult Guardian

X—NO ONE UNDER 17 ADMITTED
(Age limit may vary in certain areas)

AUDIBLE State the Rating Symbol Letter
"RATED G," "RATED PG," "RATED R," "RATED X."

Note: The visual code information (MPAA Seal, Rating Symbol
and Full Definition) should be included when the title of the
film comes on the screen and remain for *four* seconds.

RADIO SPOTS

There is little difference in acceptable content between TV
and radio spots. Most radio spots are acceptable provided
reasonably decent language is used and no cursing—the use of
the Lord's name—sex-oriented or other rough language is used.
Many stations in the middle west will not accept vulgar references
to racial or national groups. These should be avoided. In general
advertisers should be guided by good taste and use language in
radio spots that is acceptable to family audiences.

REGULATIONS FOR RADIO SPOTS
60-30-20 Second Spots

State the Rating Symbol—(G, PG, R, X)
State the Abbreviated Definition
Abbreviated Definition:

"RATED G—GENERAL AUDIENCES"
"RAGED PG—PARENTAL GUIDANCE SUGGESTED"
"RATED R—UNDER 17 NOT ADMITTED WITHOUT PARENT"
"RATED X—UNDER 17 NOT ADMITTED"

10 Second Spots State Rating Symbol Only:
"RATED G," RATED PG," RATED R," RATED X."

GENERAL INFORMATION ON RATED FILMS

A. Re-issues:

Table 5-2. MPAA Rules and Regulations (continued from page 47).

If a film is a re-issue, it must be mentioned directly or inferred in the advertising to avoid confusion and comply with the Federal Trade Commission, i.e., "now you can see again," "brought back by popular demand," "a (company name) re-release."

ALL ADVERTISING FOR A RE-ISSUE MUST BE RE-SUMBITTED

B. Title Change:

Same rule applies for a re-issue. The former title must be mentioned in all advertising, such as "formerly released as."

ALL ADVERTISING FOR A TITLE CHANGE MUST BE RE-SUBMITTED .

Special Note:

Please be advised that film titles in the recent past that have included such words as "sex," "porno," "whore," and similar strong words as part of the movie title have resulted in the film's title being changed because of the number of problems encountered with newspapers across the country.

C. Kiddie Shows:

The only trailers that should be shown during a kiddie matinee are trailers for future kiddie matinee features.

D. Double Bill:

One a double bill where each feature had a different rating, only the more restrictive of the two ratings should be used in advertising. The more restrictive rating governs box office admittance.

E. Teaser Ads:

No mention of the rating need be in a teaser ad unless the theatre where the film will be playing is mentioned. If the theatre is noted in the ad, it must show a rating.

F. Sneak Preview:

When a film is sneaked, for everyone's protection, the rating must be in the ads.

G. Foreign Language Films:

If a foreign language film is released with sub-titles, it must state this in all advertising, i.e., (French Film—English subtitles).

If a foreign language film is released in two versions, English and foreign, it must differentiate in the advertising which version is playing.

H. Rating Change:

If your film has been re-rated by the Code and Rating Administration, all advertising must reflect the change in rating.

Table 5-2. MPAA Rules and Regulations (continued from page 48).

It is advised that words such a "original," "uncut," not be used in the ad campaign. The change in rating cannot be exploited upon.

I. Distributor Changes:

If you have recently acquired a film carrying an MPAA rating, please notify us so that we can adjust our record accordingly. Also, if you change your name, address or telephone number, we would appreciate your advising us for future correspondence.

J. Posting ("wild," etc.):

Posters seen in public places other than theatres are subjected to great criticism. Therefore, it is most important that these posters are approved before use and are inoffensive.

K. "G" rated films:

Phrases such as, "for the whole family" or "family entertainment," cannot be used in any advertising unless the film has received a "G" rating.

L. New Campaigns:

If an ad campaign that has already been approved is revised or changed or a second campaign substituted, any new advertising must be submitted.

STANDARDS FOR ADVERTISING
The principles of the Code cover advertising and publicity as well as production. There are times when their specific application to advertising may be different. A motion picture is viewed as a whole and may be judged that way. It is the nature of advertising, however, that it must select and emphasize only isolated portions and aspects of a film. It thus follows that what may be appropriate in a motion picture may not be equally appropriate in advertising. Furthermore, in application to advertising, the principles and standards of the Code are supplemented by the following standards for advertising:

■ Illustrations and text shall not mispresent the character of a motion picture.
■ Illustrations shall not depict any indecent or undue exposure of the human body.
■ Advertising demeaning religion, race, or national origin shall not be used.
■ Cumulative overemphasis on sex, crime, violence and brutality shall not be permitted.
■ Salacious postures and embraces shall not be shown.
■ Censorship disputes shall not be exploited or capitalized upon.

STANDARDS FOR TITLES
■ A salacious, obscene, or profane title shall not be used on motion pictures.

Table 5-2. MPAA Rules and Regulations (continued from page 49).

AREAS IN ADVERTISING MOST SENSITIVE TO CRITICISM:
- SEX
- VIOLENCE, WEAPONS (i.e., gunsites)
- LANGUAGE and GESTURES
- NUDITY
- DRUGS and PARAPHERNALIA (i.e., needles)
- DEFAMATION (person or place, i.e., cities)
- ETHNIC or MINORITY GROUPS
- SACRILEGE
- CHILD ABUSE
- CRUELTY TO ANIMALS
- BODY FUNCTIONS
- ASSASSINATION
- VENEREAL DISEASES
- MUTATIONS
- PHYSICAL HANDICAPS (i.e., amputations)
- CADAVERS (i.e., eyes opened, abuse)
- RAPE and MOLESTATION
- LAVATORY or LAVATORY JOKES

All advertising material must contain the rating received by the MPAA. The rule is as follows: "That any and all advertising and publicity, including press books, still photographs, posters, lobby card design, trailers and radio and television spots used in any manner in connection with the advertising and exploitation of this picture shall be submitted for approval to the Director of the Code for Advertising and that only such advertising or publicity material approved by the Director shall be used in advertising and exploiting the picture hereby approved."

It should be emphasized that all material should be submitted in its early preparation stages and always before it is used by theatres or the media. The G, PG and R ratings are registered with the United States Patent Office as certification marks of the Motion Picture Association of America, Inc. Their unauthorized use, or their misuse in any way, will be subject to legal action.

The Advertising Code Regulations of the Motion Picture Association of America, Inc. are found in Table 5-3. The necessary rating from the MPAA should be obtained before accessories are made. The seal (Fig. 5-1) must appear on the front of the motion picture, the trailer, the pressbooks, the one sheet, the ads, television and radio trailers and spots. Trailer tags (Table 5-4) must remain on the theatre screen for at least five seconds.

If a producer is very wise, he will show the rough cut of his film (prior to final dubbing and cut negative) to the MPAA. If he wants a certain rating and is refused, he can then re-cut the film without too much difficulty and conform to their suggestions,

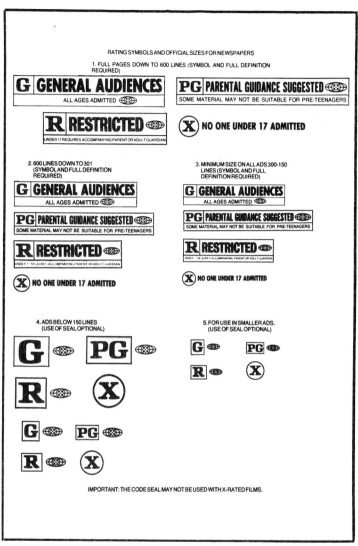

Fig. 5-1. Rating symbols.

thereby getting the rating he desires. However, once the negative on the film is cut and the producer has re-recorded the film and made the optical tracts and the answer prints, it becomes rather expensive to re-edit, re-dubb and re-cut.

Unfortunately, by the time the distributor gets the picture, the producer has made the total answer print and that is the start of expensive work. It becomes one of those 'if only' situations. 'If only

Table 5-3. Advertising Code Regulations.

ADVERTISING CODE REGULATIONS.

1 These regulations are applicable to all members of the Motion Picture Association of America, to all producers and distributors of motion pictures with respect to each picture for which the Association has granted its Certificate of Approval or Rating Certificate and to all other producers and distributors who apply the X rating to their motion pictures and voluntarily submit their advertising.

2 The term "advertising" as used herein shall be deemed to mean all forms of motion picture advertising and exploitation and ideas therefore, including the following: pressbooks; still photographs; newspaper, magazine and trade paper advertising; publicity copy and art intended for use in pressbooks or otherwise intended for general distribution in printed form or for theater use; trailers; posters, lobby displays and other outdoor displays, advertising accessories, including heralds and throwaways; novelties; copy for exploitation tieups; and all radio and television copy and spots.

3 All advertising for motion pictures which have been submitted to the Code and Rating Administration for approval and rating, or for rating only, shall be submitted to the Director of the Code for Advertising for approval before use, and shall not be used in any way until so submitted and approved. All print advertising shall be submitted in duplicate, particularly pressbooks.

4 The director of the Code for Advertising shall proceed as promptly as feasible to approve or disapprove the advertising submitted.
The Director of the Code for Advertising shall stamp "Approved" one copy of all advertising approved by him and return the stamped copy to the Company which submitted it. If the Director of the Code for Advertising disapproves of any advertising, the Director shall stamp the word "Disapproved" on one copy and return it to the Company which submitted it, together with the reasons for such disapproval; or, if the Director so desires, he may return the copy with suggestions for such changes or corrections as will cause it to be approved.

5 The Director of the Code for Advertising shall require all approved advertising for pictures submitted to the Code and Rating Administration by members of the Motion Picture Association of America and their subsidiaries to carry the official Code seal and a designation of the rating assigned to the picture by the Code and Rating Administration. Uniform standards as to type, size and prominence of the display of the seal and rating will be set forth by the Advertising Code Administrator.

6 Approved advertising for pictures submitted to the Code and Rating Administration by companies other than members of the Motion Picture Association of America, and their subsidiaries, for Code approval and rating, or for rating only, may bear the official seal at the distributor's option, but all such advertising shall bear the assigned rating.

7 Approved advertising for pictures rated X by the Code and Rating Administration shall bear the X rating but may not bear the official seal.

8 All pressbooks approved by the Director of the Code for Advertising shall bear in a prominent place the official seal of the Motion Picture Association of America and a designation of the rating assigned to the picture by the Code and Rating Administration. The word "Approved" shall be printed under the seal. Pressbooks shall also carry the following notice:

> All advertising in this pressbook, as well as all other advertising and publicity materials referred to herein, has been approved under the Standards for Advertising of the Code of Self-Regulation of the Motion Picture Association of America. All inquiries on this procedure may be addressed to:

**Director of Code for Advertising
Motion Picture Association of America.**

9 Appeals. Any Company whose advertising has been disapproved may appeal from the decision of the Director of the Code for Advertising, as follows:

It shall serve notice for such appeal on the Director of the Code for Advertising and on the President of the Association. The President, or in his absence a Vice President designated by him, shall thereupon promptly and within a week hold a hearing to pass upon the appeal. Oral and written evidence may be introduced by the Company and by the Director of the Code for Advertising, or their representatives. The appeal shall be decided as expeditiously as possible and the decision shall be final.

On appeals by companies, other than members of the Motion Picture Association of America and their subsidiaries, the President shall, if requested, decide the appeal in consultation with a representative of Int'l. Film Importers and Distributors of America, as designated by its Governing Board.

10 Any company which has been granted a Certificate of Approval and which uses advertising without securing the prior approval of the Director of the Code for Advertising or if such advertising does not include the assigned rating may be brought up on charges before the Board of Directors by the President of the Association. Within a reasonable time, the Board may hold a hearing, at which time the company and the Director of the Code for Advertising or their representatives, may present oral or written statements. The Board, by a majority vote of those present, shall decide the matter as expeditiously as possible.

If the Board of Directors finds that the company has used advertising for a Code approved and rate picture without securing approval of the Director of the Code for Advertising, or without including the assigned rating, the Board may direct the Code and Rating Administration to void and revoke the Certificate of Approval granted for the picture and require the removal of the Association's seal from all prints of the picture.

11 Each company shall be responsible for compliance by its employees and agents with these regulations.

Table 5-4. Trailer Tags.

ALL TAGS ARE TO REMAIN ON THE SCREEN FOR FIVE (5) SECONDS

THERE ARE (2) HEAD TAGS WHICH INDICATE
FOR WHICH AUDIENCE THE TRAILER IS INTENDED.

THIS SPECIAL **PREVIEW**
HAS BEEN APPROVED
FOR
ALL AUDIENCES
BY THE
MOTION PICTURE ASSOCIATION
OF AMERICA

THIS **PREVIEW**
HAS BEEN APPROVED
FOR
RESTRICTED AUDIENCES ONLY
BY THE
MOTION PICTURE ASSOCIATION
OF AMERICA

THERE ARE (4) END TAGS WHICH DESIGNATE
THE RATING OF THE FEATURE BEING ADVERTISED

THIS **MOTION PICTURE** HAS BEEN RATED

BY THE
CODE AND RATING ADMINISTRATION

THIS **MOTION PICTURE** HAS BEEN RATED

BY THE
CODE AND RATING ADMINISTRATION

THIS **MOTION PICTURE** HAS BEEN RATED

BY THE
CODE AND RATING ADMINISTRATION

THIS **MOTION PICTURE**
HAS BEEN RATED

Ⓧ **NO ONE UNDER 17 ADMITTED**

AGE LIMIT MAY VARY
IN CERTAIN AREAS

I had done this'....'If only I had done that,.... it would have been a
block-buster', etc. etc. etc. The instructions and rating symbols
must be adhered to in order to have the motion picture ready for
marketing.

OBTAINING THE MPAA RATING

If the distributor has a pre-planned release schedule, the delay
in getting the rating could be to his advantage. The MPAA sees
hundreds of films and the producer and/or distributor must wait

Table 5-5. Submittal Form for a Motion Picture Rating.

CODE AND RATING ADMINISTRATION
of the
Motion Picture Association
8480 Beverly Boulevard, Los Angeles, California 90048

(213) 643-2200

SUBMITTAL FOR RATING   Date................................

1. Title of picture ....

2. Number of reels.................Footage ....

3. Production Company ....

4. Picture produced in U.S.A. (Give Locales).......................
   and/or Foreign Country ....

5. Picture to be distributed by ....

6. Person to whom Certificate of Rating should be mailed....
   (Producer or Distributor or Representative)

....
(Address)

Copy to: West Coast Representative of Distributor/
Producer ....
                                          (If none, so state)

....
(Address)

Copy to: East Coast Representative of Distributor/
Producer ....
                                          (If none, so state)

....
                                              (Address)

Copy to: Advertising Agency...
                                          (If none, so state)

....
                                              (Address)

Copy to: Company preparing titles ....
(If none, so state)

....
(Address)

7. To Whom should invoice for certificate be sent: ....

....
(Address)

8. As to the motion picture hereby submitted, the undersigned undertakes and agrees, during the time this application is pending, and at all times thereafter, if a Certificate of Rating is granted:

(A) To submit, or cause to be submitted, to the Advertising Code Administration of the Motion Picture Association all advertising and publicity matter in connection with the advertsing or exploitation of the picture, including material for press books, still photographs, poster and lobby card designs radio and TV spots and trailers, and to use, or permit the use of, only such as have been approved by said Advertising Code Administration.

(B) To treat as confidential all communications to and from the Code and Rating Administration or the Advertising Code Administration.

(C) To inform the Code and Rating Administration of all title changes.

9. The finished picture will be submitted for final review to the C.A.R.A. at the above address. Before the picture is screened, the following must be presented to C.A.R.A.:

(A) A completed and signed submittal form.

(B) Payment by check for fee based on the fee schedule as shown on reverse side hereof. The appropriate fee category must be checked.

(C) Official credit sheet giving names of the producer, director, writers of original and screenplay, and principal characters of the cast.

(D) Brief synopsis of the story—three copies.

Table 5-6. Film Classification Fee Schedule.

I	**C.A.R.A. FEE** * **Check appropriate category:**
Class I-A Negative cost * $15,000,000 or over..............	$8,000.00 ( )
Class I-B Negative cost * $10,000,000 to $14,999,999.	$7,000.00 ( )
Class I-C Negative cost * $5,000,000 to $9,999,999.......	$6,000.00 ( )
Class I-D Negative cost * $3,000,000 to $4,999,999.......	$5,000.00 ( )
Class I-E Negative cost * $1,500,000 to $2,999,999.......	$4,000.00 ( )
Class I-F Negative cost * $1,000,000 to $1,499,999.......	$3,000.00 ( )
Class I-G Negative cost * $500,000 to $999,999..........	$2,700.00 ( )
Class I-H Negative cost * $150,000 to $499,999.............	$2,000.00 ( )
Class I-I Negative cost * $75,000 to $149,999..............	$1,100.00 ( )
Class I-J Negative cost * less than $75,000	$ 800.00 ( )
Class I-K Short Subject (any film less than 3,000 feet in length)	$ 80.00 ( )

*Negative cost shall include a reasonable amount of the salaries and other charges of those compensated on a participation basis.

II To be used only by distributors whose aggregate domestic gross film rental for the prior calendar or fiscal year was less than $2,000,000 and where the distributor has neither been involved with production activities nor participated in the financing of production.

Class II-A	Acquisition cost * $300,000 or over	$1,200.00 ( )
Class II-B	Acquisition cost * $200,000 to $299,999......	$1,100.00 ( )
Class II-C	Acquisition cost * $100,000 to $199,999......	$1,000.00 ( )
Class II-D	Acquisition cost * $50,000 to $99,999...........	$ 900.00 ( )
Class II-E	Acquisition cost * $25,000 to $49,999.........	$ 825.00 ( )
Class II-F	Acquisition cost * less than $25,000	$ 800.00 ( )
Class II-G	Where acquisition of rights is on a "straight distribution deal" which is arranged only after the completion of the film in which no cash payments or guarantees are involved...	$ 800.00 ( )

*Acquisition cost includes cash payment and/or guarantee.

Re-Issue

III Any film released prior to Novemeber 1, 1968 that has not previously been rated and that is submitted for rating prior to its Re-Issue.

Class III-A	Negative cost $1,000,000 or over................	$1,750.00 ( )
Class III-B	Negative cost $500,000 to $999,999	$1,500.00 ( )
Class III-C	Negative cost $150,000 to $499,999	$1,250.00 ( )
Class III-D	Negative cost $75,000 to $149,999.............	$1,000.00 ( )
Class III-E	Negative cost less than $75,000..................	$ 800.00 ( )

Table 5-6. Film Classification Fee Schedule (continued from page 57).

IV ReRating

Any film previously rated by this office which is submitted for ReRating after it has been placed in distribution, shall be charged a review fee in the amount of....RR-$ 800.00 ( )

Submitted by: Firm Name_____

Address & Telephone_____

Person to contact with reference to advertising material, all of which must be submitted in accordance with paragraph 8(A) on front page:

Name:_____

Address & Telephone_____

I hereby certify that, to the best of my knowledge, the above information is accurate for this film.

(SIGNED)_____
(title)

until they advise them of their scheduled review after having submitted the appropriate rating form (Table 5-5). There is also a charge that the MPAA must receive prior to viewing the film and granting the rating. A film classification fee schedule (Table 5-6).

The distributor must get the motion picture print to the offices of MPAA a day ahead of the review. After the film is reviewed, they must wait until they are notified by the MPAA as to their ratings. If the producer or the distributor does not like the rating, they can inquire as to the way the rating was granted. The MPAA will advise them in writing as to the scenes necessary to delete (if they get an X or R rating) in order to conform to a PG rating, etc.

The producer or the distributor must make the necessary changes and re-submit the re-edited film to the MPAA for further review. If the MPAA feels that the producer and distributor have conformed with their suggestions, they will then give the requested rating.

Chapter 6

Motion Picture Copyrights

Before submitting the producer's motion picture to viewing audiences, the distributior shall make the necessary application to the Register of Copyright, Library of Congress, Washington, D.C. After the submittal of appropriate forms, he should insert the legend, © surrounded by a circle on the title card of the motion picture.

WHAT IS A COPYRIGHT?

A copyright is a form of protection given by the law of the United States (Title 17,U.S. Code) to the authors of literary, dramatic, musical, artistic and other intellectual works. The owner of a copyright is granted by law certain exclusive rights in his work such as:

- ■ The right to print, reprint and copy the work.
- ■ The right to sell or distribute copies of the work.
- ■ The right to transform or revise the work by means of dramatization, translation, musical arrangement or the like.
- ■ The right to perform and record the work.

WHO CAN CLAIM COPYRIGHT?

Only the author or those deriving their rights through him can rightfully claim copyright. Mere ownership of a manuscript, painting or other copy does not necessarily give the owner the right to copyright. In the case of works made for hire, it is the employer and not the employee, who is regarded as the author. There is no provision for securing a blanket copyright to cover all the works of a particular author. Each work must be copyrighted separately if protection is desired.

COPYRIGHTING MOTION PICTURES

The copyright law (Title 17, U.S. Code) lists broad classes of works in which copyright may be claimed, with the provision that these are not to limit the subject matter of copyright. Two of the classes concerning the producer and the distributor are:

■ Motion Picture Photoplays (Class L): Published or unpublished motion pictures that are dramatic in character, such as feature films, filmed or recorded television plays, short subjects and animated cartoons, musical plays and similar productions having a plot.

■ Motion Pictures Other Than Photoplays (Class M): Published or unpublished non-dramatic motion pictures, such as newsreels, travelogs, training or promotional films, nature studies and filmed or recorded television programs having no plot.

It is advisable that a film be registered. The U.S. Copyright Office in Washington, D.C. is unable to find a registration for Woody Allen's "What's Up, Tiger Lily". This oversight could possibly leave his film in the Public Domain and hard for the producers to prosecute for piracy.

Register your motion picture!

COPYRIGHT PROCEDURE FOR UNPUBLISHED WORKS

Statutory copyright for unpublished works is secured by registering a claim in the Copyright Office. For this purpose, it is necessary to forward the following:

■ APPLICATION FORM: The appropriate form (either class L or M) may be ordered from the Copyright Office (Table 6-1). All forms are supplied free of charge.

■ COPY: In the case of manuscripts of music, dramas, lectures, etc., one complete copy should accompany the application. It will be retained by the Copyright Office in Washington, D. C. For motion pictures and photographs, instructions as stated on the application forms must be followed.

This procedure is very important. There are many cases of motion picture piracy and one should take as many precautions as possible in protecting creative properties. The right in a work will be permanently lost unless all published copies bear a notice of copyright in the form and position described later in this chapter. When a work has been published without notice of copyright, it falls into the public domain and becomes public property. After that happens it serves no purpose to add the notice of copies of the work, and doing so may be illegal.

In the case of works that cannot be registered in advance of publication, it is the act of publication with notice of copyright, rather than registration in the Copyright Office, that secures statutory copyright. While the Copyright Office registers claims to copyright, it does not grant copyright protection.

If the film has previously been published and the distributor and producer want to take steps to secure and maintain statutory copyright in a published work, they must:

■ Produce copies with copyright notice by printing or other means of reproduction. It is essential that all copies bear a copyright notice in the required form and position.

■ Publish the work by showing the film in a legitimate motion picture theatre.

■ Register a claim in the Copyright Office. This is accomplished promptly after publication by forwarding the following information to Register of Copyright:

Application form: The appropriate form is either Class L or M.

Copies: Send two copies of the best edition of the work as published.

It is best to avoid sending 35 mm prints since they are very expensive. It may be possible, if necessary, to send the 35 mm prints and request the Library of Congress to return the prints after registration. It is much better to send 16 mm prints or two videotapes of the film, whichever would be the least expensive.

FORM OF THE COPYRIGHT NOTICE

As a general rule, the copyright notice (Table 6-2) should consist of three elements:

■ The word "copyright", the abbreviation "Copr." or the symbol ©. Use of the symbol © may have advantages in securing copyright in countries that are members of the Universal Copyright Convention.

Table 6-1. Application Form for a Copyright.

Application
for Registration of a Claim to Copyright
in a motion picture

Instructions: Make sure that all applicable spaces have been completed before you submit the form. The application must be **SIGNED** at line 10. For published works the application should not be submitted until after the date of publication given in line 5 (a), and should state the facts which existed on that date.

Pages 1 and 2 should be typewritten or printed with pen and ink.

Mail all pages of the application to the Register of Copyrights, Library of Congress, Washington, D.C. 20559, together with:

(a) If unpublished, title and description, the registration fee of $6.

(b) If published, two complete copies, description, the registration fee of $6.

Make your remittance payable to the Register of Copyrights.

1. Copyright Claimant(s) and Address(es): Give the name(s) and address(es) of the copyright owner(s). For published works the name(s) should ordinarily be the same as in the notice of copyright on the copies.

Name _____

Address _____

Name _____

Address _____

2. (a) Title: _____
(Give the title of this particular motion picture as it appears on the copies)

(b) Series Title: _____
(If work is part of a series with a continuing title, also give series title)

3. (a) Nature of Work: (One of the following boxes **MUST** be checked.

☐ Class L—Photoplay   ☐ Class M—Motion picture
other than a photoplay

Table 6-1. Application Form for a Copyright (continued from page 62).

(b) Running Time or Footage: _____

4. Author: Citizenship and domicile information must be given. Where a work is made for hire, the employer is the author. The citizenship of organizations formed under U.S. Federal or State law should be stated as U.S.A. If the copyright claim is based on new matter (see line 6) give information about the author of new matter.

Name_____ Citizenship _____

(Name of country)_____

Domiciled in U.S.A. Yes___No___Address_____

NOTE: Leave all spaces of line 5 blank unless your work has been PUBLISHED.

5. (a) Date of Publication: Give the complete date when copies of this particular work were first placed on sale, sold, or publicly distributed. The date when the motion picture was made or exhibited should not be confused with the date of publication. NOTE: The full date (month, day and year) must be given.

_____
　　　(Month)　　　　　(Day)　　　　　(Year)

(b) Place of Publication: Give the name of the country in which this particular motion picture was first published.

_____

NOTE: Leave all spaces of line 6 blank unless the instructions below apply to your work.

6. Previous Registration or Publication: If a claim to copyright in any substantial part of this work was previously registered in the U.S. Copyright Office in unpublished form, or if a substantial part of the work was previously published anywhere, give requested information.

Was work previously registered? Yes _____ No _____
Date of registration_____Registration number _____
Was work previously published? Yes_____ No _____
Date of publication_____Registration number _____
Is there any substantial **NEW MATTER** in this version? Yes__
No__If your answer is "Yes," give a brief general statement of the nature of the **NEW MATTER** in this version. (New matter may consist of compilation, abridgment, editorial revision, and the like, as well as additional cinematographic work.)

Table 6-1. Application Form for a Copyright (continued from page 63).

7. If registration fee is to be charged to a deposit account established in the Copyright Office, give name of account:

8. Name and address of person or organization to whom correspondence or refund, if any, should be sent:

Name _____ Address _____

9. Send certificate to:

(Type or print name and address)

Name _____

_____
(Number and street)

_____
(City)   (State)   (ZIP code)

10. Certification: (Application not acceptable unless signed)

I CERTIFY that the statements made by me in this application are correct to the best of my knowledge.

_____
(Signature of copyright claimant of duly authorized agent)

Application Forms

Copies of the following forms will be supplied by the Copyright Office without charge upon request:

Class A Form A—Published book manufactured in the United States of America.

Class A or B

Form A—B Foreign—Book or periodical manufactured outside the United States of America (except works subject to the ad interim provisions of the copyright law).

Form A—B Ad Interim—Book or periodical in the English language manufactured and first published outside the United States of America.

Class B

Form B—Periodical manufactured in the United States of America.

Form BB—Contribution to a periodical manufactured in the United States of America.

Class C Form C—Lecture or similar production prepared for oral delivery.

Table 6-1. Application Form for a Copyright (continued from page 64).

Class D Form D—Dramatic or dramaticomusical composition.

Class E

Form E—Musical composition the author of which is a citizen or domiciliary of the United States of America or which was first published in the United States of America.

Form E Foreign—Musical composition the author of which is not a citizen or domiciliary of the United States of America and which was not first published in the United States of America.

Class F Form F—Map.

Class G Form G—Work of art or a model or design for a work of art.

Class H Form H—Reproduction of a work of art.

Class I Form I—Drawing or plastic work of a scientific or technical character.

Class J Form J—Photograph.

Class K

Form K—Print or pictorial illustration.

Form KK—Print or label used for an article of merchandise.

Class L or M Form L-M—Motion picture.

Class N Form N—Sound recording.

- Form R—Renewal copyright.

- Form U—Notice of use of copyrighted music on mechanical instruments.

FOR COPYRIGHT OFFICE USE ONLY

Application received _____

Two copies received_____

Title and description received _____

Fee received_____

Renewal _____

Prints received_____

One copy received·_____

Table 6-2. Notice of Copyright.

Certificate

Registration of a Claim to Copyright

in a motion picture

This Is To Certify that the statements set forth on this certificate have been made a part of the records of the Copyright Office. In witness whereof the seal of the Copyright Office is hereto affixed.

Register of Copyrights
United States of America

1. Copyright Claimant(s) and Addresses(es):

Name _____

Address _____

Name _____

Address _____

2. (a) Title: _____
(Title of this particular motion picture as it appears on the copies)

(b) Series Title: _____
(Series title, if work is part of a series with a continuing title.)

3. (a) Nature of Work:

☐ Class L—Photoplay ☐ Class M—Motion picture other than a photoplay

(b) Running Time or Footage:

4. Author:

Name _____ Citizenship _____
(Name of country) _____

Domiciled in U.S.A. Yes ___ No ___ Address _____

5. (a) Date of Publication:

_____
(Month)   (Day)   (Year)

Table 6-2. Notice of Copyright (continued from page 66).

(b) Place of Publication: _____

(Name of country)

6. Previous Registration or Publication:

Was work previously registered? Yes _____ No _____
Date of registration _____ Registration number _____

Was work previously published? Yes _____ No _____
Date of publication _____ Registration number _____

Is there any substantial **NEW MATTER** in this version? Yes___
No___ If your answer is "Yes," give a brief general statement of the nature of the **NEW MATTER** in this version:

7. Deposit account: _____

8. Send correspondence to:

Name _____ Address _____

9. Send certificate to:

(Type or
print
name and
address)

Name _____
Address _____
(Number and street)

(City)	(State)	(ZIP code)

Information concerning copyright in motion pictures

When to Use Form L-M. Form L-M is appropriate for unpublished and published motion pictures which are complete and ready for projection or broadcast.

What Is a "Motion Picture"? The copyright law provides for two classes of motion pictures.

—*Photoplays* (Class L) include motion pictures that are dramatic in character and tell a connected story, such as feature films, filmed television plays, and animated cartoons.

Table 6-2. Notice of Copyright (continued from page 67).

—*Motion Pictures Other Than Photoplays* (Class M) include such films as documentaries, newsreels, travelogues, promotional films, and filmed television programs having no plot.

Unpublished Scenarios. The Copyright Office *cannot* make registration for an unpublished scenario, synopsis, format, or general description of a motion picture.

No "Blanket" Copyright. The general idea, outline, or title of a motion picture or of a filmed series cannot be copyrighted. Registration for a motion picture covers the copyrightable material in the film, but does not give any sort of "blanket" protection to the characters or situations portrayed, to future films in the series, or to the series as a whole.

Duration of Copyright. Statutory copyright begins on the date the work was first published, or, if the work was registered for copyright in unpublished form, copyright begins on the date of registration. In either case, copyright lasts for 28 years, and may be renewed for a second 28-year term.

Unpublished motion pictures

How to Register a Claim. To obtain copyright registration mail the following material to the Register of Copyrights, Library of Congress, Washington, D.C. 20559. (1) one "print" taken from each scene or act if the work is a photoplay, or at least two "prints" taken from different sections of the film if not a photoplay. These "prints" may be frames or blow-ups of a film, or, if on videotape, snapshots from a studio monitor; (2) separate title and description (synopsis, press book, continuity, etc.); (3) an application on Form L-M; and (4) a fee of $6.

Procedure to Follow if Work Is Later Published. If the work is later reproduced in copies and published, it is necessary to make a second registration, following the procedure outlined below. To maintain copyright protection, all copies of the published work must contain a copyright notice in the required form and position.

Published motion pictures

What Is "Publication"? Publication, generally, means the sale, placing on sale, or public distribution of copies. In the case of a motion picture, it may also include distribution to film exchanges, film distributors, exhibitors, or broadcasters under a lease or similar arrangement.

How to Secure Copyright in a Published Motion Picture:

Table 6-2. Notice of Copyright (continued from page 68).

1. *Produce copies with the copyright notice.*
2. *Publish the work.*
3. *Register the copyright claim* by sending to the Copyright Office: (1) two complete copies of the "best" edition of the motion picture; (2) a separate description (synopsis, press book, continuity, etc.); (3) an application on Form L-M; and (4) a fee of $6. The best edition of a motion picture is generally the most widely distributed gauge, in color if available. Videotape: In addition to *two* copies of the videotape the Copyright Office requires a set of photographic reproductions from the tape including: (a) the title; (b) the copyright notice; (c) production, performance, and creativity credits; and (d) two scenes from different sections of the work.

The Copyright Notice. In order to secure copyright in a published work, it is essential that the statutory copyright notice should appear on all copies at time of first publication. This notice should consist of the word "Copyright," the abbreviation "Copr.," or the symbol ©, accompanied by the name of the copyright owner and the year date of publication. Example: © John Doe 1974. The copyright notice should be embodied in the motion picture, preferably in or near the title frames, and should be clearly seen when projected or broadcast. Use of the symbol © may result in securing copyright in countries which are parties to the Universal Copyright Convention.

NOTE: If copies are published without the required notice, the right to secure copyright is permanently lost and cannot be restored.

Return of Deposit Copies. The deposit copies (i.e., films or videotapes) of published motion pictures are subject to retention by the Library of Congress. However, it may be possible to enter into a contract with the Librarian for the return of the copies under certain conditions, and contract forms may be obtained on request. Information regarding the contract may be obtained from the Exchange and Gift Division, Library of Congress, Washington, D.C. 20540.

FOR COPYRIGHT OFFICE USE ONLY

Application received _____

Prints received_____

One copy received_____

Two copies received_____

Title and description received _____

Fee received _____

■ The name and address of the copyright owner, or owners.

■ The year and date of publication. This is ordinarily the year in which copies are first placed on sale, sold, or publicly distributed by the copyright owner or under his authority. However, if the work has previously been registered for copyright in unpublished form, the notice should contain the year and date of registration for the unpublished version. Or, if there is new copyright matter in the published version, it is advisable to include both the year and date of the unpublished registration and the year and date of publication. These three elements should appear together on the copies in this manner: © XYZ PICTURES 19 .

LENGTH OF COPYRIGHT PRODUCTION

A new law has just been enacted registering the term of the statutory copyright of the author for his lifetime . However, for practical purposes, it must be assumed that the first term of statutory copyright runs for 28 years. The term begins on the date the work is published with the notice of copyright, or, in the case of unpublished works registered in the Copyright Office, on the date of registration. A copyright must be renewed for a second term of 28 years if an acceptable renewal application and fee are received in the Copyright Office during the last year of the original term of copyright, which is measured from the exact date on which the original copyright began. Several acts of Congress have extended second term copyrights that would have expired on or after September 19, 1962. However, these extensions have no effect on the time limits for renewal registration.

INTERNATIONAL COPYRIGHT PROTECTIONS

If a work is by an author who is neither a citizen nor a domiciliary of the United States and the work is first published outside the United States, special conditions determine whether or not the work can be protected by U.S. Copyright. Specific questions on this subject and questions about securing protection for U.S. works in foreign countries, should be addressed to the Register of Copyrights, Library of Congress, Washington, D.C. 20540. Also, general information regarding international copyright matters is contained in Circular 38 furnished by the Register of Copyrights. The Register will also furnish on request current lists showing the copyright relations of various countries.

TRANSFER OR ASSIGNMENT OF STATUTORY COPYRIGHT

A copyright may be transferred or assigned by an instrument in writing, signed by the owner of the copyright. The law provides for the recording of transfers of copyright in the Copyright Office. The original signed instrument should be submitted for the purpose of recording. It will be returned following recordation. For effective protection, an assignment executed in the United States should be recorded within three months from the date of execution. Assignments executed abroad should be recorded within six months.

Chapter 7

Sub-Distributors

The distribution areas of the United States are divided into many territories. In the case of independent distributors, they have *sub-distributors*, or *exchanges*, who handle certain parts of these territories. There are overlapping states and territories where several exchanges may cover one or more states. Probably, the most misunderstood portion of motion picture distribution is the breakdown of territories to the exchanges.

The sub-distributor, or exchange, works for the distributor on a commission basis. The exchanges book the motion picture in their territory and they are very familiar with exhibitors. Exchanges usually receive a 25 percent commission for distributing the film. This 25 percent comes after deductions of advertising expenses—from local theatre newspapers and campaign—and is based on the net cash received. This will be dealt with extensively in chapter 11.

Major film distributors also have exchanges but these exchanges are really the employees of the major distributor. However, they basically perform the same services as the independent sub-distributor except that the major exchanges do not receive a commission. They are paid directly by the parent company on a salary basis.

SUB-DISTRIBUTION AGREEMENT

The motion picture distributor has an agreement with his sub-distributors not unlike the distribution agreement made with the producer. The main difference is that the distributor can cancel the exchange quite easily whereas the agreement made with the producer is quite binding.

The distributor furnishes the exchanges with all advertising material and all necessary motion picture prints. This material, of course, is for the account of the producer.

A sample sub-distributor's agreement made with a distributor is found in Table 7-1.

Before we proceed in marketing, it is very important to understand a general relationship of territories to exchanges.

EXCHANGES IN U.S. TERRITORIES

The following pages list the exchanges covering various territories in the United States including Hawaii and Alaska. Also included is information on Puerto Rico and Canada. Guam is considered the same as Hawaii and Alaska.

Figure 7-1 is a map indicating the location of the exchanges and a status of release of key and sub-key cities broken down into divisions. The exchanges are listed East to West and North to South. This breakdown is important to the student and professional and should be studied. It enables one to see visually the location and function of each exchange. Keep this list in a file for quick and easy reference.

New England Exchange

Offices usually located in Boston, Massachusetts and covering the following states:

- Maine
- New Hampshire
- Vermont
- Massachusetts
- Rhode Island
- Connecticut

New York Exchange

Offices usually located in New York City and covering the following states:

- Southern New York State including New York City, Long Island, Westchester.
- Certain parts of Northern New Jersey.

Table 7-1. Sub-Distribution Agreement.

THIS AGREEMENT, made and entered into this day of
between (hereinafter)
referred to as "Licensor"; and

(hereinafter referred to as "Licensee").

1. LICENSE AND TERM

Licensor hereby grants to Licensee and Licensee accepts, for a term of____from the date of this Agreement, unless otherwise terminated as hereinafter provided, the exclusive license to subdistribute to exhibitors for theatrical exhibition, in 35 mm only, the following motion picture:

2. TERRITORY

The territory covered by this Agreement shall consist of the motion picture exchange territory of:
This being the territory usually served by the majority of motion picture exhcanges in the above-described territory. Licensor hereby grants Licensee the right to distribute and arrange for the exhibition of the motion picture herein specified in established theatres and drive-in theatres regularly used for the exhibition for motion pictures in the above-described territory. In the event of any dispute in reference to the territorial boundaries included in said territory, the decision of Licensor shall be final.

3. DISTRIBUTION

Licensee shall not enter into any exhibition, license, booking or other agreement with any exhibitor, or others, for the exhibition of the motion picture herein named or enter into any agreement for the adjustment or alteration thereof without first obtaining the prior approval and consent of Licensor thereto and to the terms thereof.

4. DISTRIBUTION FEE AND DEDUCTIONS

Licensee shall deduct cost of shipping prints inot Licensee's exchange off the top of all film rentals collected. Thereafter, Licensee shall retain____percent (   ), of the remainder of the collected film rentals as a distribution fee. Cost of shipping, inspecting prints and storage within the Licensee's own territory is to be borne solely by Licensee.

5. ADVERTISING

Licensee shall not agree to or enter into any cooperative or other advertising campaign or plan with any exhibitor without first obtaining the approval and consent of Licensor thereto.

Table 7-1. Sub-Distribution Agreement (continued from page 74).

6. RELEASE PRINTS

Licensor shall furnish such number of release prints as Licensee reasonably may require for the purpose hereof, said prints to be delivered to such place within the territory as Licensee designates.

The legal ownership fo the release prints and any materials delivered to Licensee hereunder shall remain with Licensor at all times and at the expiration of the term of this Agreement, Licensee shall return the same to Licensor at Licensor's address, prepaid.

It shall be Licensor's right to remove from Licensee's territory, at any time, prints that are not being solidly booked.

Licensee agrees to be responsible for the safekeeping and handling of all prints provided by Licensor. Further, Licensee agrees to collect from any theatre carelessly damaging any print the cost of necessary replacement footage. Licensee shall remit 100% of any such collections to Licensor and substitute the new footage provided to Licensee by Licensor, thus keeping all prints in first class condition, less reasonable wear.

7. REPORTS AND PAYMENTS

Licensee will furnish to Licensor every 30 days, collection reports, a billing worksheet, copies of all confirmations and billings, all box office statements received and all alterations of exhibition contracts and a report of all receipts, contracts made and business written during the preceding month. Commencing on the first month following the release of the motion picture hereunder in the territory and on each month thereafter, Licensee shall pay to Licensor during and throughout the term (and thereafter as long as any gross collections are derived from the motion picture hereunder) Licensor's share of the total gross collections derived from the distribution of the picture during the preceding month. Timely and prompt payments and prompt remittances of all of said reports, records, statements and information are of the essence of this Agreement and failure to comply therewith shall be a material default of the provisions of this Agreement. Gross collections are defined as the entire amount paid by the theatre to which the picture is rented.

Licensee will hold Licensor's share of the gross collections at all times as trustee for Licensor until Licensor shall have received the same.

Table 7-1. Sub-Distribution Agreement (continued from page 75).

8. RECORDS

Licensee shall keep and maintain, at its principal place of business until the expiration of Licensee's License as set forth in paragraph I, and for a period of three (3) years thereafter, complete, detailed and accurate books of account and records relating to its sub-distribution of the motion picture herein named, including box office receipts, bookings thereof, rentals received and/or due and to become due therefrom, gross collections derived therefrom and pladates thereof and the location of prints, trailers, accessories and other material in connection with such picture.

Licensee further agrees to give to Licensor or its representatives access, at any time during regular business hours, to its records of all bookings, rentals and receipts derived from the sub-distribution, exhibition and exploitation of the motion picture and to permit the making of copies or extracts therefrom.

9. ADVANCES

As a guarantee of performance and for other reasons, Licensee agrees, with the execution of this Agreement, to advance to Licensor an amount of $_____. This advance is to be recouped by Licensee from film rental received, out of_____% of Licensor's share; but Licensee shall report each engagement and settlement promptly as provided for in paragraph 7 herein.

10. GENERAL CONDITIONS

The License herein granted is personal to Licensee. Licensee may not assign, mortgage, pledge or encumber, directly or indirectly or by operation of law, or in any other way part or attempt to part with the License, prints or accessories of any motion picture hereunder without the Licensor's prior written consent. If Licensee becomes insolvent or makes any assignment for the benefit or creditors or if a voluntary or involuntary petition in bankruptcy is filed by or against Licensee, or any amount hereunder is payable is not promptly paid when due or there is any other violation or breach by Licensee or any of its agreements made herein, or if Licensee discontinues the distribution of any motion picture herein named, the Licensor shall have the right to terminate this Agreement and all of Licensee's rights hereunder by giving written notice thereof to Licensee by Certified Mail.

Table 7-1. Sub-Distribution Agreement (continued from page 76).

Nothing contained in this Agreement shall be construed as constituting a joint venture or partnership between the parties hereto and neither party shall have the authority to bind the other as its representative in any manner whatsoever unless otherwise expressly provided in this Agreement.

Notwithstanding anything to the contrary contained elsewhere in this Agreement, this Agreement and the term hereof may be terminated by either Licensor or Licensee upon serving thirty (30) days advance written notice thereof by Certified Mail or Telegraph upon the other party hereto. In the event of any termination, whether by reason of the normal expiration of the term hereof or otherwise, all sub-distribution and other rights of Licensee in the motion picture mentioned herein automatically shall revert to Licensor, and the Licensee agrees promptly thereafter to deliver to Licensor all prints, trailers, film material and advertising accessories of the motion picture in his possession or under its control at the time of termination.

Licensor agrees to affect collections of all film rentals promptly after the close of each and every engagement. In the event that legal suit to affect collections for film rentals due may be necessary, legal fees of such suits or any other collection procedures shall be deducted off the top of film rentals.

All notice, statements and payments herein provided for or under this Agreement shall be addressed to each party hereto at the respective address specified below its signature hereto or to such other address as either party in writing may hereafter designate to the other.

IN WITNESS WHEREOF, the parties to this Agreement have set their hands the day and year first above written.

(Licensor) _____ (Licensee) _____

By: _____ By: _____

ADDRESS: ADDRESS:

_____ _____

_____ _____

_____ _____

_____ _____

Buffalo Exchange:

Offices usually located in Buffalo, New York and covering the following part of New York: north of Albany, which is the dividing line.

■ Northern New York State. This includes all of New York State north of Albany.

Philadelphia Exchange

Offices usually located in Philadelphia, Pennsylvania and covering the following states:

■ Southern part of New Jersey
■ Eastern half of Pennsylvania
■ Sometimes the northern part of Delaware

Washington D.C. Exchange

Offices usually located in Washington, D.C. or Baltimore, Maryland and covering the following states:

■ Southern part of Delaware.
■ Maryland
■ Washington, D.C.
■ Virginia

Charlotte Exchange

■ North Carolina
■ South Carolina

Atlanta Exchange

Offices located in Atlanta, Georgia and covering the following states:

■ Georgia
■ Florida
■ Alabama
■ Eastern Tennessee (Memphis, Tennessee is the dividing line)

New Orleans Exchange

Offices located in New Orleans, Louisiana and covering the following states:

■ Western Tennessee (Memphis, Tennessee is the dividing line)
■ Mississippi

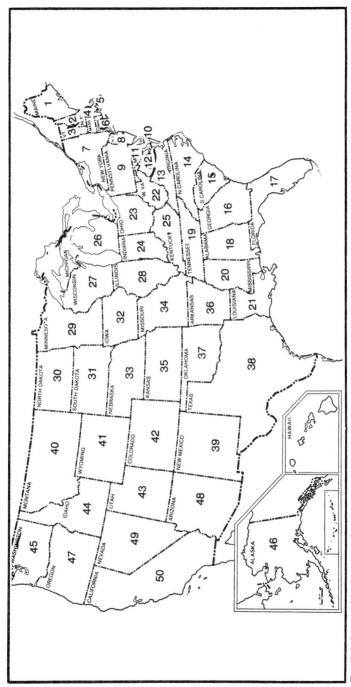

Fig. 7-1. A map of the location of exchanges.

■ Louisiana

Note: Arkansas is usually handled out of the New Orleans Exchange, but most big theatre bookings are out of Dallas and consequently, Arkansas appears in the Dallas exchange.

Cincinnati Exchange

Offices located in Cincinnati, Ohio and covering the following states:

■ Western part of Pennsylvania, including Pittsburgh.
■ West Virginia
■ Southern part of Ohio (Columbus, Ohio is the dividing line)
■ Indiana
■ Kentucky

Cleveland Exchange

Offices located in Cleveland and covering the following state:
■ North part of Ohio (Columbus, Ohio is the dividing line)
Note: Although on the surface this may look like a small exchange, it is a highly concentrated area with a large population within a number of large cities. It is an excellent box office area.

Detroit Exchange

Offices located in Detroit, Michigan and covering the following state:
■ Michigan

Chicago Exchange

Offices located in Chicago, Illinois and covering the following states:

■ Wisconsin
■ Illinois

Minneapolis Exchange

Offices located in Minneapolis, Minnesota and covering the following states:

■ Minnesota
■ North Dakota
■ South Dakota

Kansas City Exchange

Offices located in Kansas City, Missouri and covering the following states:
- Iowa
- Nebraska
- Missouri
- Kansas

Dallas Exchange

Offices located in Dallas, Texas and covering the following states:
- Arkansas
- Oklahoma
- Texas
- New Mexico

Denver Exchange

Offices located in Denver, Colorado or Salt Lake City, Utah and covering the following states:
- Montana
- Wyoming
- Colorado
- Utah
- Idaho

Note: Salt Lake City can also be an exchange, but for this book it is considered to be in the Denver Exchange.

Seattle Exchange

Offices located in Seattle, Washington and covering the following states:
- Washington
- Oregon
- Alaska

Los Angeles Exchange

Offices located in Los Angeles, California and covering the following states:
- Arizona
- Nevada

- California (southern part)
- Hawaii
- Guam

San Francisco Exchange

Offices located in San Francisco, California and covering the following states:
- California (northern part)
- Nevada (western part)
- Oregon (southern part)

Puerto Rico

Although this is a possession of the United States, all sales to Puerto Rico are considered foreign sales.

Canada

Although it is possible to have a Canadian Exchange to cover this country, it is basically considered a foreign sale.

These exchanges are to be used as a guide for study. In the case of large major distributors, there is a more extensive coverage of the territories. However, in the case of independent distributors, these listed exchanges are more than sufficient to cover the territories listed.

At this time, the independent film distributor has not quite reached the state of the art in motion picture distribution where he is able to book directly to a theatre. Occasionally, an independent can book directly but these cases are rare. These listed exchanges book for him and they usually get a fee of 25 percent commission on the net sales, after advertising expenses have been deducted.

It is hoped that, in the future, the distributor will be able to book directly. It saves the producer a 25 percent commission off the top and it also gives the distributor complete control over his bookings and print shippings. A quasi-type of theatre booking is possible whereas the distributor books directly to key theatres throughout the United States. After this key booking, the film can then be given to sub-distributors who book re-runs and smaller theatres. This type of distribution is ideal and requires a comprehensive knowledge of theatres and a decent distribution organization.

Chapter 8

Motion Picture Release Prints

As pointed out in Chapter 7, there are 19 sub-distributors or exchanges that an independent distributor has available to him. This information is vitally important since it will establish the number of *release theatre prints* the distributor will require from the film laboratory.

It can be seen immediately that, logically, each exchange will require one print for screenings to theatres in their areas. This means a total of 19 prints will be required prior to actual theatre exhibitions. The exchanges will be booking from the 19 prints.

A certain amount of *floating prints* must be projected. These prints are necessary for multiple bookings in large cities such as New York, Chicago, Detroit, Los Angeles, San Francisco, Atlanta, etc.

Remember that motion picture release prints are very expensive and the cost of these prints are for the account of the producer. This cost is deducted from his share of the profits. Additional prints can always be ordered from the film laboratory. However, if too many prints are made, they can't be returned!

For round figures, project an initial 10 floating prints. If the distributor happens to have to play several multiples at one time, he can always ship prints from the small and inactive exchanges and then return them after the playdates are finished.

From this analysis, the conclusion may be made that the distributor will initially require a maximum of 29 prints from the film laboratory. These prints give the distributor total coverage of the United States. If the motion picture proves extremely popular, then additional prints can be ordered. However, if the distributor wants to save print costs, they have the option of going first to large exchanges like New York and California. They can play their multiples there and after this has transpired, ship the extra prints to various exchanges. It is possible in this case to distribute the film with a minimum of 19 prints. However, the distributor must keep in mind that film laboratories give a price break at 24 motion picture release prints. States such as Montana, Idaho, Wyoming, North Dakota, South Dakota, Nebraska, Nevada, Utah, Arizona and New Mexico can receive prints at a later date since they represent large areas with small populations and, subsequently, less box office grosses.

Once the distributor determines the amount of release prints required, the order is made from the film laboratory. These prints are mounted and placed in shipping cans ready for shipment. Many states, like California, charge a sales tax. It is, therefore, wise to have the film laboratory ship the prints out of California, thereby avoiding unnecessary sales tax.

As you can see, the distributor now has an idea as to the amount of prints required. However, he does not order the prints as yet, but merely alerts the film laboratory as to how many prints will be needed. The distributor will first test the motion picture in a small market, such as Phoenix, Salt Lake City or Denver. This will be dealt with in Chapter 10.

PRINTS UNDER CONTROL OF THE DISTRIBUTOR

It must be assumed that all exchanges are honest. However, to avoid any conflict of double bookings—or hidden bookings—the control of all prints must be in the hands of the distributor. It would be very foolish, indeed, to ship prints directly to the sub-distributor and leave the prints in that exchange under his control. Also, one must realize the legal implications. If the exchange entered into bankruptcy, the court could freeze all of those assets, including the producer's prints. This would involve a hassle with affidavits of ownership and possible court costs. In addition, the distributor wants an accurate record of all theatres which have played the motion picture. This can only be insured by a *national film shipper* who works for the distributor, not the exchange.

A national film shipper has offices in the following cities; Albany, New York

South Boston, Massachusetts
Butte, Montana
Chicago, Illinois
Cleveland, Ohio
Denver, Colorado
Detroit, Michigan
Jacksonville, Florida
Los Angeles, California
Milwaukee, Wisconsin
New Haven, Connecticut
New York, New York
Omaha, Nebraska
Pittsburgh, Pennsylvania
St. Louis, Missouri
San Francisco, California
Washington, D.C.
Atlanta, Georgia
Buffalo, New York
Charlotte, North Carolina
Cincinnati, Ohio
Dallas, Texas
Des Moines, Iowa
Indianapolis, Indiana
North Kansas City, Missouri
Memphis, Tennessee
Minneapolis, Minnesota
New Orleans, Louisiana
Oklahoma City, Oklahoma
Philadelphia, Pennsylvania
Portland, Oregon
Salt Lake City, Utah
Seattle, Washington

Each of the above cities covers an exchange area. The exchange can make shipments within its territory by using the national film shipper's facilities. Each shipment made is charged to the distributor at a nominal cost. A record is then sent to the distributor listing the theatres and the dates the film played in that theatre.

These records are invaluable to the distributor when accounting for all theatres played. The records of the national film service can be checked against the playdate records sent to him by the sub-distributor. Additionally, all shipments outside of the sub-

Table 8-1. Conditions of Motion Picture Prints.

Term	Meaning
MINT	A new print just out of the film laboratory and never played.
1	A motion picture which is in excellent condition.
2	A motion picture in good condition.
3	A motion picture in fair condition but with extensive use.
4	A motion picture in poor condition and, at the discretion of the film distributor, on the borderline of junking.

distributor's territory can only be approved by the distributor since the national film shipper can only ship within its own area. This increases the control of prints for the distributor. This will be dealt with in more detail in Chapter 11.

MAINTENANCE OF MOTION PICTURE PRINTS

In addition to furnishing the distributor records as to where the motion picture has played, the national film shipper performs maintenance on each motion picture print as needed. He also sends in a report to the distributor explaining the condition of each print.

The terms used in the industry to describe the condition of a motion picture print are found in Table 8-1.

Most theatres will not play a film which is in number 4 condition. The distributor must keep accurate records as to the conditions of each print. In the case of a multiple run of playdates in a large city, the box office grosses will be affected if the print breaks down during projection or is so badly mutilated that it is impossible for the film to go through the film gate of the projector.

Chapter 9

Advertising and Promotion

The distributor has the option of distributing all of the accessories pertaining to the motion picture through his own organization or employing an *accessory company* who would work for the distributor on a commission basis.

ACCESSORIES

Accessories are very important and play a key role in motion picture distribution. Once a theatre books a motion picture for a definite playdate, the theatre then requests one sheets and trailers which he exhibits in his theatre several weeks in advance of the actual playdate.

If the distributor decides to distribute his own accessories he will state on the back of the pressbook that accessories are available from his company. If the distributor decides to use the services of an accessory house, this information will be printed on the pressbook.

Normally, initial printings of pressbooks will be 2000 and one sheets will also be 2000. The rule of thumb on trailers is that the distributor orders two trailers for each motion picture print ordered.

The distributor of the accessory house sells the one sheets and rents the trailers for a set fee. Many times, the income received from these sales more than pays for the cost of making the trailer and one sheets.

From a control point of view, the sales also represent a check against the sub-distributor who books the theatre. Since the theatre will want the one sheets for the front of his theatre and also want the trailer to play as a coming attraction, the distributor will know every theatre playing the motion picture. He can check the accessories orders against the sub-distributor's reports and the distributor will know if the sub-distributor leaves off a playdate.

This information, together with reports from the national film shipper gives the distributor a triple check on the activities of the motion picture film. It should be pointed out that control of all one sheets and trailers must be in the hands of the distributor. If a sub-distributor had copies of the trailers or one sheets, then he could book the motion picture into a local theatre in his exchange. The distributor would not have a copy of the one sheet or trailer request, and if the sub-distributor did not advise the distributor of the playdate, the sub-distributor could pocket the money. The only items that the sub-distributor should control are the pressbooks which are used to book the theatres. Pressbooks are shipped free to legitimate theatres and persons interested in booking the film.

The distributor may elect to use the services of an accessory house for the following reasons:

■ The distributor is not set up to handle small shipments.

■ The distributor does not want to bother with shipping, accounting and billings.

■ The distributor does not have space available for storage.

In this case, the distributor will employ the accessory house and the accessory house will make all shipments of one sheets and trailers. They will also bill and collect all monies for the rental of these items.

For this service, the accessory house receives 60 percent of the income from these sales and rentals and the distributor receives 40 percent of the income. The distributor receives either monthly or quarterly reports from the accessory house listing all theatres and incomes received from the sale of the accessories.

Table 9-1 illustrates a sample agreement between the distributor—in this case called the *producer*—and the accessory house.

COSTS OF ADVERTISING AND PROMOTIONS

It is necessary to distinguish the difference between advertising and promotion as it ties in with the pre-distribution of the motion picture, and advertising costs as they incur through physical distribution of the motion picture made by sub-distributors and exhibitors.

Many motion picture distributors are quick to say "prints and advertising are for the account of the producer." This means, all costs of prints and advertising incurred by the distributor are recouped from the producer's share of profits from the exhibition of the motion picture. This is not necessarily true.

What should be clarified is that prints and all *pre-distribution costs of advertising and promotion* are for the account of the producer. Advertising costs incurred by the exhibitor are "off the top" of box office receipts and technically the theatre exhibitor, the sub-distributors, the distributor and the producer all share in these advertising costs.

This distinction should be defined in any distribution a-greement. If not, it can lead to gross misunderstandings between the distributor and the producer. Of course, the producer will end up getting the short end of the stick.

To clarify this understanding even further, advertising costs shall include the following—no more, no less: (The producer pays for the total costs).

■ All trailers and all costs incurred in making the trailer.

■ All costs of the pressbooks, both in making and printing same.

■ All costs of the one sheets, both in making and printing same.

■ All costs of the radio and TV spots, both in making and printing same.

■ All public appearances by artists necessary to promote the film.

■ All costs of paperback or hard cover books and soundtracks, albums or theme songs which will help the sale of the motion picture.

■ All ads in trade papers promoting and advertising the film.

■ All costs in a general category incurred in the distributor, i.e. entertainment, press releases, press showings, publicity releases and other forms of media such as television shows, radio shows and personal appearances necessary to promote the motion picture.

This should all be in the advertising and promotion clause of the distribution agreement.

As indicated previously, the ad layouts for newspaper and television and radio spots are listed in the pressbook. The

Table 9-1. Accessories Agreement.

Distribution of Accessories and/or Trailers.

Agreement made this _____ day of _____ , _____

between _____ of _____
(hereinafter referred to as Producer)_____ and _____

located at _____ referred to

as _____

In consideration of the mutal agreement hereinafter

set forth, the parties hereto have agreed and do hereby

agree as follows:

1. _____ represents that they are the author-

ized producers of the motion picture (s) entitled_____

_____ (hereinafter referred to as picture

(s).

2. Producer will supply_____ with necessary accessory

material on picture, specifically, one sheets, press books

and trailers.

3. In consideration of paragraph 4 below producer hereby

grants and assigns distribution rights on the accessories

on picture to _____ for the following territory,

_____

_____

_____

4. Producer is to receive_____ of all net

sales collections (excluding postal charges reimbursed)

for the above accessories.

Table 9-1. Accessories Agreement (continued from page 90).

5. Producer will make available to _____ all 8 × 10

negatives and/or photoengravings available on the

picture (s). _____ is authorized to use said negatives

and/or photoengravings to reproduce 8 x 10 contact

prints and/or newspaper mats for distribution.

6. All revenue derived from the sale of material as,

noted in Paragraph 5 shall be retained by _____ . No

accounting therefore shall be necessary.

7. Press books where available shall be distributed free

of charge unless otherwise noted.

8. Producer agrees to supply a minimum of two

trailers per print in distribution. If bookings

exceed two per month per print, producer agrees to provide

additional trailers as necessary.

9. Producer agrees that _____ shall have complete

control of all accessories. Any shipments other than press

books made by producer will be reported to _____ for

billing and inventory control.

10. _____ will issue reports to producer on a monthly

basis commencing 90 days after the first playdate on

picture.

11. The term of this contract is for 5 years commencing

_____ , termination _____ and is can-

cellable by either party, with a written 90 day notice

delivered via U.S. mail.

Table 9-1. Accessories Agreement (continued from page 91).

12. Producer agrees, in the event this contract is

cancelled by Producer, that Producer will fully reimburse

_____ for all expenses & material purchased as a

result of this contract.

13. This agreement shall be binding upon the parties

hereto, their respective successors and assigns.

IN WITNESS WHEREOF, the parties hereto have executed this agreement on the ____ day of , ____ 19 ____ .

by	_____
_____	_____
Witness	
by	_____
_____	_____
Witness	

exhibitor will use these tools when booking the film in his theatre
and will use his own judgment in budgeting the advertising
campaign for his theatre. However, if the distributor or the
producer wants to spend more money than the budget allocated by
the exhibitor, then all additional costs will be for the account of the
producer.

This is rather confusing and the producer must have an
understanding with the distributor on all communications pertaining to advertising and promotions.

GRAPHIC ADVERTISING

Today's advertising relies on vivid graphics. Since people
read less frequently, one must capture them visually. In the case of
films other than sex or violence, the ad campaign is softer and more
blatant. One must appeal to basic instincts. The bigger the stars,
the easier the publicity. In fact, they generate their own publicity.

However, one must be careful not to scare the audience so
much that they are afraid to see the film. The less specific the ad,
the better the campaign. Eighty-nine percent of audiences 18 years
and older rely on daily newspapers as their main source of
information about motion pictures. Almost every newspaper
covers ads and press releases about the industry. One can see

immediately how important the pressbook is and how the ad campaign can make or break a film.

Television and radio spots are used in saturation campaigns. July and August are the busiest months of theatre audience attendance and Friday and Saturday are the busiest days. All campaigns should be geared to this fact. Saturday can account for up to 30 percent of the weekly gross of the theatre. Friday is next with 25 percent of the weekly gross. The other days of the week average between seven and eight percent of the gross box office.

BOX OFFICE GROSS

The only thing the motion picture distributor is really interested in is how much money he will receive from the exhibitor. This is called *film rental* or *distributor's gross*. Both mean the same thing. However, in order to promote the motion picture, the distributor will always talk about box office figures. This may be confusing to the layman but it is the highest figure. It represents total box office receipts before any deductions are made by the exhibitor for advertising or any other expense.

In line with this thinking, a motion picture distributor will exploit the film by booking an exhibitor who will be large enough to guarantee a high *box office gross* . This is done so that the distributor may take an ad in the trades (Variety or Box office, etc.). The distributor will quote the gross figure earned on the picture in that theatre. The distributor does not mention whether the theatre is booked on a 90/10% percent with floors, or a sliding scale or if they paid additional advertising over the budget. The box office gross gives an indication of the motion picture's strength at the box office. Many times, the motion picture distributor will lose money on that date due to high advertising costs. This is never indicated in the promotional release to the trades. It is better to sell the sizzle rather than the steak.

WORD-OF-MOUTH ADVERTISING

People can become walking billboards for you through word of mouth advertising.

Sneak Previews

Sneak previews can be very effective. It can build word-of-mouth advertising. However, sneak previews should only be considered when the motion picture distributor has an excellent film and he is sure that it is a winner. Sneaks must be paired with comparable pictures. For example, if the exhibitor is exhibiting an 'R' rated film, then the sneak film should be an 'R', action with action; and love story with love story.

Since Friday and Saturday nights are the best box office nights and most people attending the theatre will be there on those nights, distributors should insist the sneak be held at that time. Many exhibitors want to hipe up their slow days during the week, but this would defeat the purposes of the sneak preview. The sneak should be timed within one or two weeks of the motion picture opening.

Benefits and Charities

This is another form of sneak preview. However, in this case, it is beneficial to religious or charitable organizations. Usually, only motion pictures with big casts can go through this route. The benefit to the motion picture distributor is that sneaks and benefits are cheap. Besides the cost of nominal ads proclaiming a sneak or benefit, they are the best possible way to promote the film. This is especially true with the high costs of advertising. The theatre owners like the idea of a 'free' picture since it brings in more audiences who also like the idea of a 'free' picture.

SEASONS

There is much confusion as to when to release a motion picture. Seasons vary and holidays enter the picture. Income taxes and property taxes all affect the movie-going audiences. There are several breakdowns of the theatre seasons.

1st Quarter: January to Easter

There is a heavy fall-off from the Christmas season when many new films have played. This is an excellent film season. Thus from January to Washington's birthday-two months after Christmas-is a very bad time for film releases.

2nd Quarter: Easter through Independence Day (July 4th)

Things start picking up from Easter on. June always has early summer premieres. This is a fairly good period for film releases.

3rd Quarter: Independence Day through the first week of September

This is the best time to release films. Kids are home from school. Adults are on vacation. Television stations are showing re-runs. Drive-ins are packed due to the hot weather. It is definitely the theatre season.

4th Quarter: Early September through the Middle of December

This is the weakest season for film releases. Kids are in school, people are back from vacation and the television season is the strongest. However, just before Christmas is the emergence of the exploitation saturations of soft core porno; the horror shows; science-fiction shows; and some early exclusive runs of important films qualifying for the Academy Awards.

Sometimes, a film played in this season can do quite well due to the fact that the 'big boys' are holding their films up for better releasing schedules.

THEATRE ADVERTISING

This is usually referred to as *cooperative advertising agreements*. The exhibitor has the right to budget his own advertising and to make agreements with local advertising agencies to book the newspaper and television and ratio spots. The distributor has the right to approve or disapprove the advertising budget.

However, in most cases, the local exhibitor knows his market and realizes the potential of each film and budgets accordingly. After a playdate, the exhibitor sends his theatre reports and a copy of the advertising costs and contracts to the sub-distributor. He also sends the distributor's share of the box office receipts. Usually, the advertising costs are broken down by the advertising agency into newspaper ads, television viewing schedules and radio monitoring schedules. The distributor analyses this information in his check of theatre figures.

As stated previously, the bulk of advertising will be through newspapers and it is important for the student and the professional alike to have a knowledge of this area of advertising.

ONE COLUMN ADS VS. TWO COLUMN ADS

Why use a two column ad instead of a one column ad or vice-versa? If a competitor or many competitors are using a two column ad, an exhibitor might get a better position on the entertainment page if he used a one column ad that day.

The best position of an ad is above the fold. Most readers scan a page starting at the upper left-hand corner, following a diagonal line to the lower right-hand corner. It is, therefore, more favorable to have the ad positioned as close to the upper left corner of the page as possible.

Most newspapers build a page from the lower right-hand corner. If they start building the page with many column ads and then pyramid the columns working to the left, then the single-column ad may be on the left, atop the two column ads. An efficient exhibitor will know the head of the composing room, and, just maybe give him a pass to the theatre. He might find that he is always close to the upper left-hand corner of the amusement section.

In the case of several ads, there might be a separation of ads if the newspaper is not instructed otherwise. It is always better to group ads. It makes the ads look bigger and draws attention to the theatre.

The ads suggested in the pressbook are only that, suggested ads. Many times the local exhibitor might want to compose his own ad. He knows the area and knows the demographics.

It is wise to use a heavy line or border to enclose the entire ad. It keeps the ad in tack. It is also wise to bevel edges where possible to have clear separation from the other ads.

If ads other than theatre ads appear on the same page, the exhibitor should loudly complain to the newspaper. They might not be aware of the damage they do. There are tricks to catch the reader's eye. It is important to set the ad off from the other copy. No one can use an arrow pointing to the ad, indented borders or reverse printing. Use a lot of white space because one cannot know what ad will border the motion picture ad.

There are oversized ad borders with heavy borders. This border can be used for dominance and the ad can be placed within the border. It is wise to include the border in the ad section of the pressbook. The inside width of the borders matches the outside width of the ad in the pressbook. The exhibitor can take the borders from the pressbook.

Care should be taken when reducing art work. There are various arts such as *Ben Day* which is a series of dots or lines that combine to form a gray area. Another form of art is a line drawing which is a drawing made with pen and ink. There are also halftones. This is the breaking up of a photograph into various tones by photographing through a screen.

In all cases possible, the exhibitor should run his ads in combination. They look much larger and can result in more economical savings of advertising. It is smart business for an exhibitor to place the next coming attraction on the last week of advertising of the current film. It is very reasonable and is a teaser for the viewing audience. It is important to plant the idea that the motion picture is very popular and that the audience is lucky to see it. It pays off with box office receipts.

Imagination is very important in laying out ads. The competition is fighting for those box office grosses. Any idea that results in more income is worth considering.

The first ad, sometimes called the *announcement ad*, is the first ad to break in the newspapers. It is generally a large ad and runs on a Sunday because that day represents the largest circulation of most newspapers. The ad runs on Sunday and announces the film which will open three days later (usually on Wednesday).

All newspapers have a different style in the column structure. However, they all have the terminology of one column, two column, etc. For edification, listed are the average sizes of each column:

- One column: the width is one and three-quarters inch.
- Two column: the width is three and five-eighths inches.
- Three column: the width is five and one-half inches.
- Four column: the width is seven and one-half inches.

Notice the four column ad is more than four times larger than a one column ad and this is due to the fact that each column picks up borders normally separated per column.

Lines mean the depth or length of the page. Many ads will say 25 lines, 50 lines, 100 lines, etc. This literally means the size of the length of the ad. It has nothing to do with columns.

CROSS PLUGS

Cross Plugs can be incorporated into the advertising and promotional campaign. These plugs can be helpful in increasing the box office grosses of the motion picture as well as increasing income from the sale of hard cover or soft cover books relating to the film. A successful film can generate the sale of these books. Conversely, a successful book can generate the box office grosses of the motion picture.

In the case of sound tracks and theme songs these can be tied to radio airplays and record store displays while the film is playing in a given market. This does not insure the success of the album or theme song but most of the risk money on making the album or theme song has already been absorbed in the production of the film in recording the tracks. In fact, the sale of 2500 albums would recoup all costs for the sound track and the producer would have his money back.

If the theme song from the motion picture proves popular with recording artists this will enhance the box office grosses of the motion picture since more airplay will be used and it will tie-in with the motion picture.

Chapter 10
Accounting and Distribution Control

The primary function of the motion picture distributor is to accomplish the following:

■ Book the producer's motion picture into theatres.

■ Enter this booking on comprehensive records (cut-off sheets) in order to have maximum control of the income of the motion picture.

■ After the motion picture has played, the distributor (through his exchange) must bill the theatre.

■ Collect all monies due from exhibition earnings of the motion picture.

In order to fulfill the above, the distributor must have sufficient records to control the exchange and the theatres. The following record keeping procedures are for a very modest sized distribution company. Of course, the bigger the distribution company, the more people will be employed, and subsequently, the more control will be needed.

BOOKING AND CONTROL SHEET

The pivot for the control of theatre bookings is a form entitled *Booking and Control Sheet*. (Fig. 10-1). This form is vital to distribution control and is a printed form with various colored sheets and carbon papers inserted between the colored sheets. It is a multi-purpose form encompassing complete control of theatre playdates, exchange reports and financial distribution information.

CRICKET FILM PRODUCTION, INC.

BOOKING AND CONTROL SHEET

MOTION PICTURE: _____

STATE	EXCHANGE	CIRCUIT	PLAYDATE
TERMS	CONTROL DATE	CONFIRMATION NUMBER	
		A - 00001	

theatre _____

city and state _____

shipping date	shipping point
playdate	playdate cancelled
	date: _____

previous confirmation number _____

PLAYDATE REMARKS:

percentage ☐ yes SCALE

flat date ☐ yes AMOUNT $ _____

no. UNIT POINTS (1 to 10) _____

THEATRE REMARKS:

FLASH GROSS FROM EXCHANGE

(fill out this section and return)

BOX OFFICE GROSS ....$ _____

less:

2nd feature .... _____

advertising .... _____

other .... _____

NET INCOME TO EXCHANGE..$ _____

THEATRE DATA:

walk in drive in ☐   drive in ☐

population of city: _____

capacity _____ weather _____

number of units played: _____

RECOMMENDATIONS

REMITTANCE ADVICE

(per exchange collection/theatre report)

NET INCOME
(settled at .... $ _____

less:

advertising .... _____

freight .... _____

screenings .... _____

misc. ( ) .... _____

exchange commission .... _____

other .... _____

TOTAL NET INCOME .... $ _____

NET REMITTED .... $ _____

TOTAL DEPOSTIED AMOUNT ....$ _____

COMMENTS:

Fig. 10-1. Booking and control sheet.

Once the exhibitor books the motion picture through the exchange, varied procedures are put in motion through the use of the Booking and Control Sheet.

SUB-DISTRIBUTOR'S BOOKING ADVICE

The motion picture distributor is advised of bookings through his exchanges in many varied forms. However, there is a semi-standard form which is used by most of the exchanges.

Figure 10-2 is an example of this booking advice form. Notice on the blank form that the exchange lists the following information:

■ The name of the producer. In reality, this is the name of the distributor.

■ The date of the booking notice.

■ The name of the circuit (theatre owners or booking agents).

■ The name of the theatre.

■ The town and state of the theatre.

■ The name of the motion picture.

■ The shipping date. This date is always ahead of the actual playdate and it shows the last date possible to ship the print to meet the playdate schedule.

■ The playdate.

■ Prior date cancelled. If the film had been cancelled previously they will list the previous playdate.

■ Terms. Listed are the financial arrangements the exchange made with the theatre. The terms are either a percentage of the gross income or a flat price.

■ Advertising and remarks. Here the exchange advises if there is advertising on the film and what arrangements are made for sharing this advertising.

The forms will vary but will contain the same essential information necessary for the motion picture distributor to understand the booking playdate. If he desires, he can either approve or disapprove the playdate booking at this time.

A hypothetical booking date has been entered on a sub-distributor's booking advice form in Fig. 10-3. Certain procedures are put in motion upon receipt of the form. Once the motion picture distributor receives the advice form, it is the responsibility of the distributor's *booking and control clerk* to enter the information on the *booking and control sheet* and to incorporate varied other entries which will be discussed at length.

PRODUCER _____

ABC SUB-DISTRIBUTION CO. IN.
_____ 10000 COMEMERCE STREET, SUITE 110
DALLAS, TEXAS

DATE _____

CIRCUIT	THEATRE	TOWN AND STATE	PICTURE	SHIP DATE	PLAYDATE	PRIOR DATE CANCELLED	TERMS	ADVERTISING & REMARKS

Fig. 10-2. A sub-distributor's booking advice form.

ABC SUB-DISTRIBUTION CO. INC.
10000 COMMERCE STREET, SUITE 110
DALLAS, TEXAS

PRODUCER: CRICKET FILMS

BRANCH ___ DALLAS

DATE: October 1

CIRCUIT	THEATRE	TOWN AND STATE	PICTURE	SHIP DATE	PLAYDATE	PRIOR DATE CANCELLED	TERMS	ADVERTISING & REMARKS
Johnson	Skyview DI	Dallas, Tex.	TOUCH OF HEAVEN	10/18	10/20–27		25%	co op

Fig. 10-3. A hypothetical booking date on a sub-distributor's booking advice form.

The exchange must list all vital information necessary and the booking and control clerk must study the advice form to make sure that he receives a comprehensive booking.

FUNCTIONS OF BOOKING AND CONTROL CLERK

On all initial bookings (per booking advice sheet), the booking and control clerk fills out only the information contained in the booking advice sheet sent to him by the exchange.

This information is entered on the booking and control sheet by the clerk (Fig. 10-4). The information will be typed since there are many sheets attached and each sheet will eventually go to different departments of the distribution company. Each department will be coded by a colored page. However, all forms will be exact duplicates of each other.

The booking and control clerk is responsible for initiating the information on the booking and control sheet. Also, he keeps an accurate record of the location of the motion picture prints. He also makes sure that each playdate recorded has an available print. If not, he orders a print from another exchange to make the playdate.

INTERNAL OFFICE DISTRIBUTION

The booking and control clerk must distribute the booking and control sheets. He must also advise all departments if a playdate is cancelled.

White Copy (top sheet)

The booking and control clerk forwards the completed section of the booking and control sheet to the sales manager of the distribution company for approval of the playdate and booking terms are not favorable to him, he will directly advise the exchange and send a copy of this advice to the booking and control clerk. If the sales manager approves the booking he initials the white sheet and files the booking and control sheet under the confirmation number listed on the sheet in numerical order for future reference.

Blue Copy (2nd page of form)

The booking and control clerk sends the blue copy of the booking and control sheet to the master control division of the distribution company (home office). The master control division enters the information on a master sheet and then files the booking and control sheet in numerical order per the confirmation number on the booking and control sheet. Later, the master control

CRICKET FILM PRODUCTIONS, INC.

BOOKING AND CONTROL SHEET

MOTION PICTURE: TOUCH HEAVEN

	STATE	EXCHANGE	CIRCUIT	PLAYDATE
	TEXAS	ABC SUB-DISTRI	JOHNSON	10/20-27
	TERMS	CONTROL DATE	CONFIRMATION NUMBER	
	25%	10/1/	A-00001	

theatre
   Skyview DI

city and state
   Dallas, Texas

shipping date	shipping point
10/18	Dallas, Texas
playdate	playdate cancelled
10/20-27	date:

previous confirmation number
   None

PLAYDATE REMARKS:

percentage [x] yes SCALE _25%_

flat date [ ] yes AMOUNT $_____

no. UNIT POINTS (1 to 10) _____

THEATRE REMARKS: Co-Op advertising

FLASH GROSS FROM EXCHANGE

(fill out this section and return)

BOX OFFICE GROSS ......$ _____

less:
2nd feature ....
advertising ....
other ....

NET INCOME TO EXCHANGE ..$ _____

THEATRE DATA:

walk in [ ]   drive in [ ]

population of city: _____

capacity _____ weather _____

number of units played: _____

RECOMMENDATIONS:

REMITTANCE ADVICE

(per exchange collection/theatre report)

NET INCOME
(settled at) ....$ _____
less:
advertising ....
freight ....
screenings ....
misc. (............)
exchange commission ......
other ....

TOTAL NET INCOME ......$ _____

NET REMMITTED ......$ _____

TOTAL DEPOSITED AMOUNT .$ _____

COMMENTS:

Fig. 10-4. A sample booking and control sheet partially filled in by a booking and control clerk.

division will check this blue copy with the final deposit slip and collection report (which will be accompanied by a totally filled out green sheet after full collection).

After sending out the white and blue copy of the booking and control sheet, the booking and control clerk posts the playdate on his print control booking sheet. This posting shows the print number and the day of the week and the date of the month. The booking and control clerk will immediately see if he has sufficient prints to fill the playdate. If not, he will advise another exchange or order another print from storage or the film laboratory. All of this is, of course, with sales manager's approval.

The print control booking sheet is also vitally important to the distributor (Fig. 10-5). All entries on this form are made in Pencil in case of a hold-over or theatre cancellation.

The exchange also keeps a print control booking sheet but it is to the advantage of the distributor to control each exchange since he is looking at a national overall picture of the prints. The local exchange is looking only into their own needs.

If the booking and control clerk orders additional prints for this playdate, he notes this information on the inventory control card file. This is a card index file. Each card is 3 x 5 inches and filed by print number rather than by exchange. In this way, the print is more important. All the booking and control clerk has to do is move the card from one exchange to another merely by taking the card out of the section of one exchange and moving it to another section of another exchange. This is minimum work and has tremendous control.

The inventory control card file (Fig. 10-6) is a rather simple form listing the motion picture and print number. Print conditions are judged by standard numbers running one through four. It is an important communication link in the motion picture distribution industry. Number one in this case means mint condition—usually never before played. On initial playdates where great amounts of advertising dollars have been spent some large theatres demand a number one print. Number two means a good print. It has been run previously but has limited scratches and the sprocket holes are not pulled or torn. Number three means a fair print which is almost marginal. It has been repaired and has some scratches but the sprocket holes are still in fair condition. A number four is a marginal print. Most decent theatres won't take a number four print under any conditions. It should be junked.

CRICKET FILM PRODUCTIONS, INC. MOTION PICTURE: __TOUCH OF HEAVEN__

PRINT CONTROL BOOKING SHEET

EXCHANGE: __ABC SUB-DISTRIBUTING CO. INC.__   MONTH OF: __OCTOBER__

DAY OF WEEK	DATE OF MONTH	PRINT NO. 501	PRINT NO.	PRINT NO.	PRINT NO.	PRINT NO.	PRINT NO.	PRINT NO.	PRINT NO.
W	1								
T	2								
F	3								
S	4								
S	5								
M	6								
T	7								
W	8								
T	9								
F	10								
S	11								
S	12								
M	13								
T	14								
W	15								
T	16								
F	17								
S	18								
S	19								
M	20	SKYVIEW D1							
T	21								
W	22								
T	23								
F	24								
S	25								
S	26								
M	27	SKYVIEW D1							
T	28								
W	29								
T	30								

Fig. 10-5. A print control booking sheet.

```
┌─────────────────────────────────────────────────────────────────┐
│                                                                   │
│  CRICKET FILM PRODUCTION. INC        INVENTORY CONTROL CARD FILE  │
│                                                                   │
│  MOTION PICTURE _____ PRINT NO. _____         │
│                                                                   │
│  print condition   (1)  excellent   (2)  good  (3)  fair.  (4)  poor │
│  ┌──────────┬───────────┬────────────┬───────────┬─────────┐     │
│  │ LOCATION │ DATE REC D │ DATE SHIP D │ CONDITION │ REMARKS │     │
│  ├──────────┼───────────┼────────────┼───────────┼─────────┤     │
│  │          │           │            │           │         │     │
│  ├──────────┼───────────┼────────────┼───────────┼─────────┤     │
│  │          │           │            │           │         │     │
│  ├──────────┼───────────┼────────────┼───────────┼─────────┤     │
│  │          │           │            │           │         │     │
│  ├──────────┼───────────┼────────────┼───────────┼─────────┤     │
│  │          │           │            │           │         │     │
│  ├──────────┼───────────┼────────────┼───────────┼─────────┤     │
│  │          │           │            │           │         │     │
│  └──────────┴───────────┴────────────┴───────────┴─────────┘     │
│                                                                   │
└─────────────────────────────────────────────────────────────────┘
```

Fig. 10-6. Inventory control card file.

PRINT INVENTORY RECORD BOOK

Final duties of the booking and control clerk include keeping accurate records of all the prints in his possession as well as those prints sent out to the various exchanges. He keeps this record on a form entitled print inventory record book (Fig. 10-7). It is a comprehensive history of all the prints and contains the following information:

- Name of the motion picture.
- Running time of the film.
- Print number.
- Date shipped.
- Acknowledged receipt of print at location.
- Date received at the location.
- Date shipped from that location to a new location.
- Name of the new location.
- Date confirmed and received at the new location.

These records are extremely important in that motion picture prints are very expensive and without complete control of their locations, they become lost quite easily and quickly.

It requires constant checking with the exchanges since many times their records are inadequate and they will demand more prints than are required for their playdates. This, of course, is an added expense for the distributor and the producer.

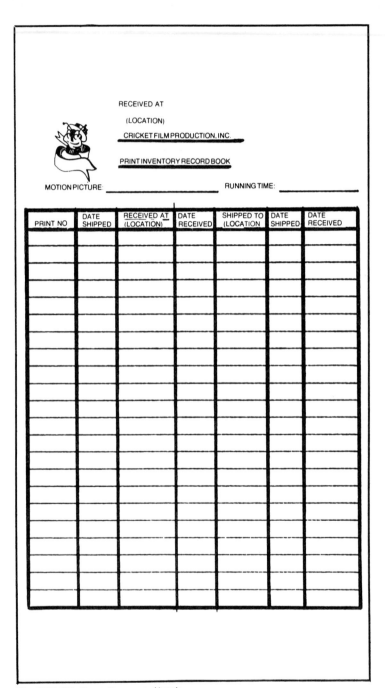

Fig. 10-7. Print inventory record book.

Perfect control of the prints will enable the distributor to run a smooth operation without unnecessary and expensive telephone calls and frantic anxieties on the part of the exchange and the distributor.

It also prevents theft and temptations on the part of unscrupulous persons awaiting any signs of a disorganized distribution company.

The booking and control clerk will advise the sales manager, master control division and accounts receivable if a playdate is cancelled. He will also amend his print records accordingly.

DUTIES OF THE ACCOUNTS RECEIVABLE DEPARTMENT

After sending out the white copy of the booking control sheet to the sales manager, sending the blue copy to master control and making the appropriate print recordings, the booking and control clerk sends the remaining copies of the booking and control sheet onto the accounts receivable department for their appropriate action.

After receipt of the booking and control sheet (less the white and blue copies), the accounts receivable department files this form in a suspense film in chronological order per the date and month of the playdate indicated on the booking and control sheet. No further action will be taken on this form until after the motion picture has played. This is due to the fact that unless the picture actually plays a theatre date, it is not considered an account receivable. Also, there is the possibility that the start of the playdate may be extended or even cancelled.

FLASH GROSS FROM EXCHANGE

If, prior to the playdate, the accounts receivable department is not advised of a cancellation or an extended playdate, then, on the last day of the playdate the accounts receivable department sends out the flash gross copy of the booking and control form to the exchange. The exchange is to fill out as much information as possible on the flash gross sheet (Fig. 10-8). The exchange gets the gross from the theatre either by telephone call or a theatre memo giving the gross income received during the playdate. The flash gross sheet is the orange copy (3rd page) of the booking and control form.

Information required on the flash gross sheet is very simple yet it will give the accounts receivable department an estimated account receivable. The flash gross from the exchange lists the following necessary information:

Box Offices Gross: This is the gross income that the theatre made through sales of tickets at the box office on the motion picture.

Less The Second Feature: When a film plays percentage (referred to as top of the bill), the picture playing flat (referred to as bottom of the bill) is paid a net price. This net price is paid out of the box office receipts and this flat price is deducted from the box office sales. When a picture plays flat it is guaranteed that flat price regardless of what the percentage film grosses. Flat prices can vary but they usually run anywhere from $50.00 to $250.00, depending on the motion picture and the contract.

Advertising: As indicated on the booking advice form, there is cooperative advertising on this film. The distributor's share of this advertising is deducted from the box office gross.

Other: This item covers multiple combinations of deductions, i.e. personal appearance expenses; unique theatre displays; and other deductions which might arise. This term is also deducted from the box office gross of the theatre.

Net Income To Exchange: This represents the remaining figures after all deductions have been made from the box office gross.

All of the above figures are merely a guideline since it will take some time for the theatre to figure the total advertising expenses and certain deductions. The flash gross is approximate and will be a ballpark figure only.

Theatre Data: This is for the information of the distributor on future bookings. The distributor should know if the theatre is a walk-in or a drive-in; the population of the city; the capacity of the theatre; and the weather conditions at the time the film was playing. It is important in an analysis of the playdate.

Number Of Units Played: This is a different standard of measurement which is peculiar to theatre accounting. It means that generally all theatres arrive at a point of measurement which gauge the daily box office gross of the theatre. The normal unit for a week's playdate is gauged at 10 and the weekends, i.e. Friday, Saturday and Sunday are allocated two units each day for a total of six units. Monday, Tuesday, Wednesday and Thursday are each allocated one unit. This is important when you analyze a playdate. If the motion picture only played for three days, one must know the units allocated to each particular day. For example, if you played Wednesday, Thursday and Friday, you would arrive at a four unit playdate. Whereas, if the picture played Saturday and Sunday only, you would also arrive at a four unit playdate. This information

EXHIBITOR'S REPORT OF PERCENTAGE ENGAGEMENT

PLEASE FILL IN ALL INFORMATION AND **SIGN AND RETURN BOTH WHITE AND PINK** COPIES IMMEDIATELY UPON CLOSE OF THE ENGAGEMENT WITH YOUR CHECK FOR FILM RENTAL DUE.

```
                                          DATE
                                          PICTURE
                                   TOUCH OF HEAVEN
                                          PLAY DATE
                                   10/20-27
                                   SECOND FEATURE (IF ANY
      ┌                     ┐      SPACE    $50.00
                                          RENTAL TERMS
        Skyview DI                 GUARANTEE $
                                   PERCENTAGE DETAIL
        Dallas, Texas              SCALE 25%

      └                     ┘
```

EXHIBITOR OR CIRCUIT _____ Johnson _____

FOLD HERE

D A Y	DATE AND WEATHER	T R C O K E L	NUMBER OF TICKETS SOLD AT NET PRICES INDICATED (EXCLUDING TAX)										DAILY AND TOTAL RECEIPTS	
			TICKET NOS.	TOTAL SOLD	TICKET NOS.	TOTAL SOLD	TICKET NOS.	TOTAL SOLD	TICKET NOS.	TOTAL SOLD	TICKET NOS.	TOTAL SOLD		
S U N	15	CLOSE / OPEN		41									118	08
M O N	16	CLOSE / OPEN		34									97	92
T U E	17	CLOSE / OPEN		37		6							123	84
W E D	5/11	CLOSE / OPEN		29		27							161	88
T H U	12	CLOSE / OPEN		49		32							233	28
F R I	13	CLOSE / OPEN		45		41							247	68
S A T	14	CLOSE / OPEN		29		12							112	08
M O D		CLOSE / OPEN												
TOTALS													1100	16

AUTHORIZED DEDUCTIONS FOR		50.00
TOTAL AUTHORIZED DEDUCTIONS		50.—
NET GROSS		1050 16
SPLIT FIGURE		
FILM RENTAL CALCULATION		
25 % OF $		262 54
% OF $		
TOTAL % EARNINGS (RENTAL)		
LESS GUARANTEE (DATE BILLS)		74 61
AMOUNT DUE		187 93

CERTIFIED AS CORRECT BY:

THEATRE CASHIER _____

EXHIBITOR _____

Fig. 10-8. A sample exhibitor's report of percentage engagement from the Skyview Drive-In, Dallas, Texas.

enables the distributor to understand the gross income and make or approve terms accordingly.

Recommendations: All recommendations received will be valuable to the distributor since he will be playing that theatre again in the future.

After the playdate of the motion picture, the booking and control sheet, less the white, blue and orange copies will be placed in the accounts receivable file awaiting payment from the theatre and the exchange.

When the accounts receivable department receives the flash gross sheet from the exchange, they forward this flash gross sheet to the sales manager after they record the information on the remaining booking and control sheets.

The sales manager will study the information on the flash gross sheet and if he is satisfied with the results he will file this orange copy with his white copy and await the remittance results.

While the accounts receivable department awaits payment on this playdate, they send out monthly reports listing all accounts receivables. They also include the confirmation number on the booking and control sheet. These reports show 30, 60 and 90 days overdue.

The sales manager and the master control division receive copies of these reports for their information and knowledge.

THEATRE AND COLLECTION REPORTS

After a theatre has completed a playdate, the manager makes out an exhibitor's report of percentage engagement. Figure 10-8 is such a report from the Skyview DI, Dallas, Texas. This is a small theatre and as a result they made only a fair amount of box office gross.

On this exhibitor's report of percentage engagement the theatre has indicated the following information:

The picture: Touch of Heaven
The playdate: 10/20-27
The second feature: Space
The rental terms: Scale 25%
The name of theatre: Skyview DI
The circuit: Johnson

This information is usually on top of the average exhibitor's report. Usually in the middle section of the report the date and weather; number of tickets sold (excluding tax) and the daily and total receipts for the playdate are listed. The Skyview DI report indicates a total box office gross of $1100.16 for the full 10 unit playdate (seven days).

The bottom half of the exhibitor's report form is usually reserved for deductions and computations. Deductions of the Skyview DI are found in Table 10-1.

The Skyview DI supports the advertising deduction by sending along a breakdown of the cooperative advertising campaign (Fig. 10-9). This cooperative advertising campaign is a rather simple campaign geared for newspaper advertising only. This form lists the days the picture was advertised, the number of lines to the page and the rate per line. The total cost of newspaper advertising came to $149.23.

Since this is a cooperative advertising campaign, the exhibitor contributes $74.62 and the exchange contributes $74.61. This amount of $74.61 was deducted from the exchange's share of film rental.

No broadcasting was spent nor was there any television advertising.

All theatres must support the deduction of the advertising by sending a copy of costs of the advertising campaign with their theatre report.

PERCENTAGE SALES

At this point, you must be wondering exactly how a theatre computes the 25 percent percentage scale.

Table 10-1. Skyview DI Deductions.

Total Box Office Receipts	$1100.16 (total income from ticket sales)
Less second feature "Space"	50.00 (deducted from box office gross for account of percentage playdate (top bill)
Net Gross	$1050.16
Film Rental Calculation	262.54 (producer's share 25% of $1050.16 per agreement of scale 25%)
Less 50% (co-op) Advertising	74.61 (per booking agreement co-op)
Amount Due	$187.93 (paid to the exchange)

AAA   ADVERTISING AGENCY, INC.
3529 Shields Boulevard
Dallas, Texas

Picture:	TOUCH OF HEAVEN
Theatre:	Skyview DI
Playdate:	10/20-27

NEWSPAPER

& Times:

DAY	DATE	LINES	RATE	AMOUNT

Journal:

DAY	DATE	LINES	RATE	AMOUNT
Wed	5/11	96	.39	37.44
Thur	12	96	.39	37.44
Fri	13	96	.39	37.44
Sat	14	23	.39	8.97
Sun	15	22	.49	10.78
Mon	16	22	39	8.58
Tue	17	22	.39	8.58

& Times _____ lines @ _____ = $ _____ + _____ lines @ _____

= $ _____ Total _____ & Times .... $ _____

Journal 355 lines @ .39 = $ 138.45 + 22 lines @ .49

= $ 10.78 + _____ lines @ _____ = $ _____ Total Journal .... $ 149.23

Agency Layout Fee, _____ lines @ _____ per line, Total .... $ _____

Other Newspaper: _____ $ _____

Total Newspace .... $ _____

Broadcast:

$ _____

Grand Total Campaign ----------------------------------- $ _____

74.61

Fig. 10-9. Cooperative advertising campaign form.

All theatres have a certain overhead which is constant. They must do enough box office gross to pay for that overhead. In the case of drive-in theatres, they have a summer and a winter scale. When the exchange books a theatre, the theatre advises the exchange of their particular break-down costs on a weekly basis. They usually give inflated figures so it is very difficult to earn more than 25 percent.

The theatre also omits the fact that they make as much money selling popcorn as they do exhibiting the motion picture.

Theatres advise the exchange of their sliding scale. The Skyview DI of Dallas, Texas advised their exchange that they use the sliding scale in Table 10-2.

It becomes quite obvious that A Touch of Heaven didn't do too well in the Skyview DI. The theatre will claim it lost money during this playdate since their breakeven revenue must be $2690.00 for the seven days. Since A Touch of Heaven only did $1100.16, the theatre settled at the 25 percent minimum scale.

In reference to the sliding scale, theatres base their computations on units of 10. If A Touch of Heaven played only on Friday,

Table 10-2. Sliding Scale Breakdown of the Skyview DI.

Percentage	Revenue
25%	$2690.00
26%	2750.00
27%	2820.00
28%	2880.00
29%	2960.00
30%	3030.00
31%	3120.00
32%	3200.00
33%	3300.00
34%	3400.00
35%	3510.00
36%	3620.00
37%	3750.00
38%	3890.00
39%	4040.00
40%	4620.00
41%	4810.00
42%	5000.00
43%	5210.00
44%	5444.00
45%	5690.00
46%	5970.00
47%	6270.00
48%	6610.00
49%	6980.00
50%	7400.00
51%	7870.00
52%	8410.00
53%	9020.00
54%	9740.00

Saturday and Sunday, this would give the exchange a total of six units. Since this would be a six unit playdate, divide ten into the figure of $2690.00—the 25 Percent minimum. This figure would come to $269.00 per unit. Therefore, A Touch of Heaven would have to do six times $269.00 in order to qualify for the 25 percent scale.

Some theatres base their sliding scale on units of 11 when their Saturday is carried as a three unit day. In these cases, you must divide their weekly dollar break-even costs by 11. Other theatres list their break-even costs minus the last digit. Although the above sounds complicated, it is quite simple once the reader does several exercises by computing the actual sliding scale. Unless exceptionally well received, most playdates will be settled at the 25 percent minimum scale.

COLLECTION REPORT

After the exchange receives the exhibitor's report of percentage engagement and the breakdown of costs of the cooperative advertising campaign, he checks all the additions for any errors. If there are none, he accepts the check from the theater. The exchange then sends his own collection report to the distributor. Each report is different from each exchange but essentially the same information is noted.

In the case of the playdate at the Skyview DI, Dallas, Texas, the exchange was ABC Sub-Distribution Co. Inc. They sent in their collection report (Fig. 10-10) together with their check in the amount of $136.95 which represents the distributor's share of the income from the exhibition of the motion picture at the Skyview DI. Their collection report is simple, as most of them are. It lists the following minimum information:

- To the distribution company.
- Date of collection report.
- Name of theatre playing the picture.
- Town and state of the theatre.
- The motion picture in question.
- The playdate.
- The net film rental received by the exchange from the theatre exhibitor.
- Shipment charge. This is the cost of shipping the film from the film depot to the theatre. In this case, the charge was $4.00 for the shipment.

116

ABC SUB-DISTRIBUTION, INC.
10000 COMMERCE STREET, SUITE 110
DALLAS, TEXAS

C O L L E C T I O N   R E P O R T

TO:

FILM PRODUCTION   DATE: Dec. 1

THEATRE	TOWN & STATE	PICTURE	PLAYDATE	NET FILM RENTAL
Skyview DI	Dallas, Texas	A TOUCH OF HEAVEN	10/20-27	187.93

1 shipment at 4.00 = $ 4.00

COLLECTIONS:

LESS DISTRIBUTORS SHARE, 25% 46.98

LESS SHIPPING:
LESS ATTACHED:

PRODUCER   136.95

CDI 4

Fig. 10-10. A sample collection report.

CRICKET FILM PRODUCTIONS, INC.   ACCOUNTS RECEIVABLE CONFIRMATION NUMBER CONTROL SHEETS   MOTION PICTURE _____

LOCATION	THEATRE	CIRCUIT	PLAYDATE	TERMS	GROSS RECEIPTS	ADVER-TISING	OTHER EXPENSE	NET FILM RENTAL	DATE PAID	DEPOSIT DATE	EXCHANGE	CONFIRMATION NUMBER

Fig. 10-11. Accounts receivable confirmation control sheets.

■ Collections. This is the total amount collected from theatre exchange.

■ Less sub-distributor's share: In this case, the exchange deducts 25 percent of the monies received by the theatre which comes to $46.98.

■ Less Shipping. In this case, the charge of $4.00 is deducted from the distributor's share.

■ The producer. In reality, the distributor. This is the net income to the distributor from the playdate. This amount should match the sub-distributors check.

Once the accounts receivable department receives the collection report as well as the exhibitor's report of percentage engagement and the breakdown of costs of the cooperative advertising campaign from the exchange, they initiate the following:

■ Pull the booking and control sheets from the accounts receivable file and check the terms and playdate against the reports.

■ Check the computations and additions to ascertain that all figures are correct.

■ Fill out the balances of the booking and control sheets and make their entries on their own internal records.

■ Make the necessary bank deposit slip and attach the bank deposit slip to the green copy of the booking and control sheet and send same to the master control. Both the green copy and off white copy bears a paid stamp and dated.

■ Pass the remaining copy of the booking and control sheet onto the sales manager. This copy is off white and is more like the consistency of a 3 x 5 card.

A recapitulation of the colors and functions of the booking and control sheet is as follows:

White copy: For sales manager's information, approval and file.

Blue copy: For master control division for general information and file.

Orange copy: For flash gross from the distributor's exchange handling playdate.

Green copy: For master control containing filled out information and bank deposit slip attached.

Off white copy: For sales manager's information and control duties. This copy has almost a card-like base consistency.

ACCOUNTS RECEIVABLE INTERNAL CONTROL

As in the case of the booking and control clerk, the accounts receivable department must have the proper forms and control. The first form (Fig. 10-11) is designed for control by confirmation number. Primarily, the master control will be by confirmation number. The secondary control will be by exchanges.

The confirmation number control form is used as a cross reference. The primary check will be that all bookings entered on the booking and control sheet are entered on the accounts receivable confirmation number control form.

Notice the confirmation number listed on the extreme right hand side of the form (Fig. 10-11). This confirmation number will be in order of the booking . Information on the form will conform exactly with the information on the booking and control sheet and will be filed in numerical order per confirmation number.

This form contains the following information:

- Name of the motion picture.
- Location (town and state of the theatre).
- Name of theatre booking motion picture.
- Name of the circuit owning theatre.
- Playdate.
- Terms.
- Gross Receipts of the theatre per theatre engagement report.
- Advertising costs per theatre engagement report.
- Other expenses. Enter the expenses listed on the theatre report and the commission paid to the exchange.
- Net film rental to the distributor after all deductions including the 25 percent commission to the exchange.
- Date Paid.
- Deposit Date.
- Name of exchange handling the film.
- Confirmation number. This number will already be on the form and must conform to the confirmation number listed on the booking and control sheet.

The secondary control sheet (Fig. 10-12) is a cross reference to the confirmation number control.

The accounts receivable exchange control sheet is basically the same as the accounts receivable confirmation control sheets. However, this form is designed for control of the exchanges rather than for the control of the confirmation numbers. Every item is identical but the filing is by exchange. Both of these forms are

CRICKET FILM PRODUCTIONS, INC. _____ ACCOUNTS RECEIVABLE EXCHANGE CONTROL SHEET   MOTION PICTURE _____

LOCATION	THEATRE	CIRCUIT	PLAYDATE	TERMS	GROSS RECEIPTS	ADVER-TISING	OTHER EXPENSE	NET FILM RENTAL	DATE PAID	DEPOSIT DATE	CONFIRMATION NUMBER	EXCHANGE

Fig. 10-12. Accounts receivable exchange control sheet.

important for analysis reasons as well as control reasons. Every quarter of the year, both of these forms should be compiled in an exchange income report form (Fig. 10-13) with copies to the sales manager and the master control. The report form is quite simple and each month is separate. The report focuses on the exchanges. This form appraises the sales manager and master control. It also enables the booking and control clerk to check each item to ascertain that the accounts receivable department is listing all of the playdates that is reported.

It is a multi-purpose control and is geared to keep all departments aware of the scope of the distribution of the motion picture.

This report lists the following:

■ Name of the motion picture. Each report is separate for each motion picture.

■ The name of the exchange which covers the motion picture and territory.

■ The reporting period, i.e. 1st quarter, 19___.

■ Month and year. This shows the accounting period and collections made in that month.

■ City and state of the playdate.

■ Name of theatre.

■ Playdates.

■ Original terms of the booking.

■ Net film rental. This is the amount that the distribution company earned after all deductions.

■ Total income earned during this particular quarter.

■ Confirmation number. Here we list the confirmation number of the motion picture booking which conforms to the booking and control sheet of the playdate.

This report enables everyone in the distribution company to be aware of the activities of the motion picture. It can be shown to the motion picture producer for his information as well. If the distribution agreement calls for quarterly reporting, this form is used for the projection of income.

ACCOUNTING FOR ACCESSORIES

All accessories (trailers and one sheets) are distributed independently from the motion picture. This distribution is by an *accessories house*. The accessories house works for the distributor on a percentage basis. The basis usually runs 60 percent of net income to the accessory house nd 40 percent of all net income to the distributor.

CRICKET FILM PRODUCTIONS, INC.   MOTION PICTURE: _____

REPORT OF EARNED EXCHANGE INCOME   REPORT NO. _____

EXCHANGE: _____   COVERING: _____ QUARTER, 19 _____

MONTH AND YEAR	CITY/STATE	THEATRE	PLAY DATES	TERMS	CRICKET'S NET FILM RENTAL	TOTAL	CONFIR-MATION NO

Fig. 10-13. A sample exchange income report form, sometimes referred to as a cut-off sheet.

The theatre orders the trailer and one sheets directly from the accessory house and the accessory house notifies the distribution via a monthly report of each theatre that rented the trailer and one sheets. They also report how much theatre rental they received. This information is communicated to the distributor on a monthly accessory report (Fig. 10-14).

This report from the accessory house is supposed to be sent to the distributor on a monthly basis. However, there are times when the accessory house is behind schedule and when this happens, they send the reports on a quarterly basis. Along with the report the accessory house sends a check to the distributor representing their shared gross. Their shared gross is 40 percent of the income received through rentals and sales.

The monthly accessory report is quite simple and covers the following items:

Account: Listed is the name of the distributor.

Period: Listed is the accounting period of the monthly accessory report.

Theatre: Listed is the name of the theatre booking or renting accessories.

City and state: Listed is the city and state of the theatre.

Title: Listed is the title of the motion picture on which the report is based.

Invoice Number: Listed is the invoice number which the accessory house used to bill the theatre.

Date paid: Listed is the date paid by theatre for accessories.

Shared gross: this figure represents the gross income received by the accessory house from theatres and is the basis of the distributor receiving his 40 percent fee.

This report is extremely important to the distributor since it will enable him to check on the exchange bookings and reports. No exchanges should have one sheets or trailers. If a theatre wants a one sheet or a trailer, the manager must advise the accessory house either by phone or mail and must pay for same. If the accessory house is honest in their reports, then the distributor will have a clear picture of each playdate and will know if any exchange omitted a theatre in their reports to the distributor.

There are times, however, where a theatre is so small that they do not want to pay for trailer rentals or one sheets. In these cases, the accessory house will not be able to report this theatre on their monthly accessory report. In that case, the exchange should

ACCT. CRICKET FILMS   PERIOD

MONTHLY ACCESSORY REPORT

Theatre	City — State	Title	Inv. No.	Date Paid	Shared Gross

Fig. 10-14. A sample monthly accessory report.

be contacted to find out what happened. This information works as a counter-check with the accessory house. This is a unique means of checks and balances. There are the theatre reports from the exchanges on the motion picture exhibition and the accessory house reports on the trailers and accessories. Two separate and distinct means of control.

This information is reflected on the final report that the accounts receivable department must make. This report is a recapitulation of all playdates and accessory house reports on the motion picture. It is a wrap-up of the motion picture distribution. It is called a recapitulation of cut-off playdates (exhibitor's record cards).

This form (Fig. 10-15) should be made semi-annually and becomes a continuous form. That is to say, the playdates are added to the form as they are finished.

This form gives the sales manager and the master control division an immediate visual record of the motion picture. It is listed by states and lists all cities with populations of over 5,000. It is a multi-purpose form and is the ultimate in control and analysis of possible markets.

There is a great deal of information listed on the recapitulation of cut-off playdates form. A breakdown of this information is as follows:

State: The form is listed by state. This increases the visual understanding of the playdates since they are not grouped together and it is easy to study the playdates in this form.

Page Number: There will be many pages on this form and this listing keeps the pages in order.

Population of city: In this column is listed all cities in the state that have a population over 5,000.

City of playdate: Here is listed the city of the playdate.

Theatre name of playdate: Here is listed the name of theatre. Also under the theatre name, the playdates are broken down into first run, second run, and third run. The first run is usually on a percentage playdate while the second and third runs are on a flat rental. Occasionally, a motion picture will go into additional runs but that is quite unlikely.

Theatre circuit booked: Listed here is the theatre circuit booked. This is taken from the information on the booking and control sheet.

Sub-distributor: Listed is the name of the sub or exchange.

128

Fig. 10-15. A sample recapitulation of cut-off playdates. This form is also called. an exhibitor's record card.

Playdates of picture: This form is designed for two pictures to be reported at once. The plan is two-fold. The sales manager can see how each picture plays against each other. Then he is in a position to talk to the exchanges and study the motion picture if it does poorly.

Net theatre income on: Under this is typed the motion picture in question.

Net access income on: Under this column all income received per the accessory house report is listed. The sales manager can immediately see if the accessory house omitted the playdate or if the theatre ommitted the playdate.

When this form is properly used it is a very important tool for evaluation and study. One must realize that the motion picture will not play in all the cities listed on the form since many cities overlap each other and one playdate can cover several cities. However, this form serves as an excellent demographic study for the sales manager and others to see the playdate possibilities.

Without all of these reports, the sales manager and the master control unit would not be able to properly distribute the films.

The accounts receivable department is burdened with many duties, particularly with all of the forms. But each duty is vitally important to the control of the distribution of the motion picture. The control which is possible in the accounts receivable department can very well carry the salaries of all employees since they will be able to police the film and avoid any lost income due to carelessness, theft or neglect.

The accounts receivable department is the foundation of the distribution company.

IN-HOUSE DISTRIBUTION OF ACCESSORIES

In the event, the distributor wishes to have complete and ultimate control of the distribution of accessories to theatres, he has the option of controlling this distribution through the facilities in his own company. There are several advantages. First, the fee of 60 percent which he pays to the accessory house is eliminated. Second, he avoids the possibility that the accessory house does not report all income. The distributor also eliminates the necessity of tightly policing the exchanges since the distributor will have direct contact with each theatre.

If the distributor elects to distribute the accessories, several procedures must be followed. As in the case of the motion picture prints, the booking and control clerk will be responsible for all accessories including the following:

130

All stills: These are 8 x 10 prints usually in black and white that fit into theatre marquis or displays in front of the theatre.

Mats: These are actually no longer in use since advance printing technology has enabled the newspapers to use the pressbook material. Previously, newspapers required soft reversd mats for ads.

One sheets: These are large ad displays running 27 x 41 inches and fitting into the theatre display frames. They are folded and ready for shipment.

Pressbooks: These are sales tools that are shipped to theatres without charge.

Trailers: These are short synopses of the films in 35 mm color running approximately two to three minutes.

The back of the pressbook will advise the theatre that accessories are available from the distributor. After booking the motion picture, the theatre will request from the distributor, either by phone or mail, certain accessories such as a trailer, or stills or one sheets. This information is recorded by the booking and control clerk on an accessory order form (Fig. 10-16). The accessory order form should be filled out in duplicate. The original will be forwarded to the accounts receivable department for appropriate billing and control. The copy is to be retained by the booking and control clerk for back up of his records. The booking and control clerk keeps petty cash on hand and will be replenished by the accounts receivable department when he submits receipts from the post office for shipment, PS form 3816 and the copy of the accessory order. The accessory order form in Fig. 10-16 is self-explanatory. All information contained in the accessory order must be recorded.

All shipments made by the booking and control clerk will be prepaid by the booking and control clerk to the Post Office. The shipments will be made C. O. D. and the U.S. Postal Authorities will reimburse the distribution company for the prepaid costs when they collect same from the theatre.

PS Form 3816 is used for all C.O.D. shipments (Fig. 10-17). Form PS 3877 (Fig. 10-18) is to be filled out by the booking and control clerk and retained in his department as a permanent record.

The booking and control clerk will send with each trailer a numbered return label for proper identification and credit to each theatre. This will be indicated on the accessory order form.

CRICKET FILM PRODUCTIONS, INC.

ACCESSORY ORDER

SOLD TO: _____ SHIP AND BILL TO: _____

(THEATRE) _____ _____

_____ _____

_____ _____

HOW ORDERED: LETTER ☐ FORM ☐ PHONE ☐ ORDERED BY:

DATE ORDERED: SHIP VIA: AIRMAIL | PARCEL POST | 1ST CLASS | SPECIAL DELIVERY

MOTION PICTURE	ONE SHEETS	MATS	STILLS	TRAILER	PRESS	SHIP DATE	PLAY DATE	NO. OF WEEKS

ORDER TAKEN BY: _____ DATE SHIPPED _____ DATE ADVISED ACCOUNTS REC. _____

DATE SHIPPED: _____ CHARGES: _____ MONEY ORDER FEE: _____

ENTERED INTO POST OFFICE FORM 3877A ON THE _____ DAY OF _____ , 19 ____

FORWARD TO THE ACCOUNTS RECEIVABLE DEPARTMENT ON THE ____ DAY OF _____. , 19 ____.

MADE OUT NUMBERED RETURN LABELS FOR RETURNED TRAILERS. YES ☐ NO ☐

Fig. 10-16. An accessory order form.

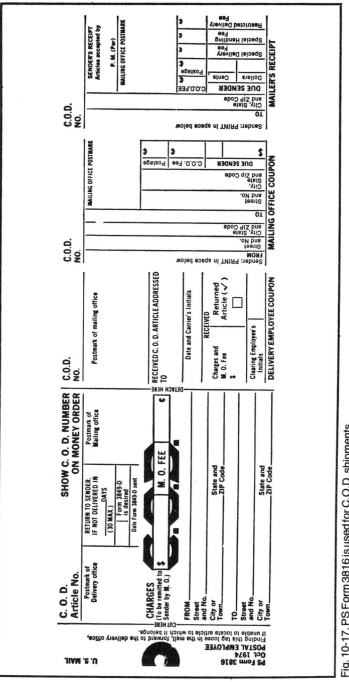

Fig. 10-17. PS Form 3816 is used for C.O.D. shipments.

133

Fig. 10-18. Form PS 3877 is retained by the booking and control clerk as a permanent record.

CRICKET FILM PRODUCTIONS, INC.,

ACCESSORY BILLING

INVOICE NO._____

DATE_____

NET: TEN DAYS

SOLD TO

SHIP TO

SHIPPED VIA	DATE SHIPPED	ACCOUNT	C.O.D.
ORDERED BY:	DATE ORDERED	METHOD OF ORDER LETTER FORM PHONE	

YOUR TRAILER ORDER IS BEING PROCESSED AND WILL BE SHIPPED   1 2 3 4   WEEKS IN ADVANCE

NOTES:

ITEMS	FEATURE TITLES			EACH	UNIT PRICE	AMOUNT
ONE SHEETS						
MATS						
STILLS						
PRESSBOOKS					N/C	
TRAILER NUMBER						
RADIO SPOTS 10 SEC. 20 SEC.						
T.V. SPOTS 10 SEC. 20 SEC.						
PLAYDATE						

IMPORTANT! RETURN TRAILER IMMEDIATELY AFTER USE. ADDITIONAL CHARGE WILL BE MADE FOR OVERDUE TRAILERS. PLEASE PAY FROM INVOICE AND REFER TO INVOICE NO. WHEN REMITTING.

SUB TOTAL	
SALES TAX	
POSTAGE	
TOTAL	

Fig. 10-19. An accessory billing invoice form.

MORE DUTIES OF THE ACCOUNTS RECEIVABLE DEPARTMENT

The accounts receivable department will be responsible for billing the theatre directly. They will use the information contained in the accessory order form forwarded by the booking and control clerk.

The accounts receivable department will also reimburse the booking and control clerk for all monies advanced on the C.O.D. shipments and will bill the theatre for this amount.

The current rates for the rental and sale of the accessory materials are found in Table 10-3.

Gentlemen:

Enclosed is our invoice no.____covering your recent order. If you received your order by C.O.D. and wish to have an open account with us, please so advise and we will adjust our records accordingly. Additionally, we would like the name of the owner and manager of the theatre for our future records.

Remember, when placing an order please state the number of weeks trailer will be used by your theatre as well as the playdate of the motion picture. If we do not know, the trailer will be shipped for two weeks. Any cancellation of a trailer already shipped, we will have to charge a handling charge of $3.45, plus postage.

Trailers are to be returned on the day the motion picture opens. Ten days are allowed for trailers to reach our office, by U.S. Mail only. Cost to be paid by the theatre. Numbered return labels received with the trailer MUST be used when returning trailer for proper identification and credit for your theatre. If the trailer is not received within this period of time, you will be billed for additional charges at the normal trailer rental rate. Remember, you will be billed for the length of time the trailer is in your possession.

We are sure you understand our feelings in this matter. We cannot rent a trailer to another theatre as long as it is still in your possession. Another theatre owner, like yourself, may suffer from this delay.
Thank you for your order and we wish you good luck on the playdate.

Sincerely,

Fig. 10-20. Accompanying cover letter with a billing invoice.

Table 10-3. Rented Accessory Materials and Their Fees.

Rented Material	Rental Fee
Color Trailers:	*First week (Minimum): $12.50 Second week: 10.00 Third week & thereafter: 7.50
One Sheets:	(outright sale)
Each sheet Stills	2.00 Depends on the number, but usually $1.00 each
Press books	Free

* The number of weeks that the trailer will be used will be noted by the booking and control clerk.

Occasionally, there will be requests for radio and TV spots and this price must be determined. It must be fair since the distributor will also increase his gross income through a good campaign.

It is very possible for the distributor to make all of his investments back plus a reasonable profit on his pressbooks, one sheets and trailers from theatre rental and sale of the accessories. Figure 10-19 is a copy of the billing form for the invoicing of these accessories. In addition to the billing invoice, a cover letter should be sent to the theatre (Fig. 10-20).

Chapter 11

Functions of the Sales Manager

Although the activities of the booking and control clerk and the accounts receivable department are operating at a peak and efficient capacity, the ultimate success of the distribution company rests with the sales manager. The sales manager wears many hats. He must be alert, intelligent, ambitious and willing to work long and hard hours. His aggressive nature stimulates the entire company and he is, in effect, the captain of the ship. Because he must deal with exchanges and theatres, he must have a wide and varied experience in motion picture distribution. Many times, the exchanges and theatres will only be contacting the sales manager. Subsequently, the reputation of the company rests on his shoulders. He must be report-conscious and demand perfection in these reports. It is his communication to the exchanges that serves as the window to the sales condition of the motion picture.

Another attribute of the sales manager must be his creativity in selling the exchanges and theatres on new approaches to advertising and sales. His relentless drive keeps the exchanges on their toes. He demands that they expend the utmost energy on the motion pictures and that they continuously look for new markets and new merchandising. His intellectual distrust of all exchanges enables him to cut through all the misty illusions of poor excuses. He is a man who deals in realities. Because of that, he is sometimes cruel...but always an administrator. He is a man who can be trusted because he demands trust in himself. He is the man who can break or make his company.

ADMINISTRATIVE DUTIES

Within the company, the sales manager must rely on the employees to be operating at a peak capacity. This allows him to expend all of his time promoting the sales of the motion pictures under his banner. In order to guarantee that these employees are, in fact, working at their peak capacity, he must be in daily contact with all of the departments. He must also chair weekly meetings between all departments to coordinate the activities of these departments and weld them into a team. They must all work together and if they understand the functions of the other departments, they will naturally gear their efforts toward full cooperation.

These weekly meetings should be the time for exploring new ideas and procedures. The sales manager must be open to all suggestions. Activities of all the exchanges should be discussed as well as conditions of the markets and discussions of the industry pertaining to motion picture distribution. Every employee should feel that his opinion counts. This is also the opportunity to inquire about any new motion picture productions and possible leads to producers desiring to have his motion picture distributed. The feeling should be one of a team effort and everyone should be encouraged to speak his piece.

Outside the company, the sales manager must be extremely social and attend many functions with other members of the distribution industry. His knowledge of projected films and promotional sales campaigns can guide the company. He should be free to exchange ideas with his peers and be willing to help others. In return, he should expect information and help. He must be well adjusted with an outgoing and easy nature open to new ideas and changes.

OFFICE PROCEDURES

The sales manager, representing the distribution company, must fulfill the role of the distributor. The primary duty is to book the motion picture into as many theatres as possible. This can only be accomplished with diligent concentration to bookings. He must check daily the bookings reported by the booking and control clerk on the booking and control form. If he approves the playdate he should initial the form and keep the form in a suspense film for his own edification and record. If he feels that the exchange is not booking sufficient theatres, it is his duty to so inform the exchange.

He has the power to cancel an exchange if he so desires and he should not hesitate to exercise this power. He should always be alert to new exchanges. Perhaps he will discover one that is more enterprising and more aggressive than the exchange currently being used.

Eventually, the sales manager will end up with excellent exchanges who are ambitious and enterprising. This will, of course, help the distribution company as well as the sales manager. He can then put his full efforts toward new products and advertising campaigns.

The sales manager should be alert to all reports on accounts receivables and discuss these receivables with the exchanges. He should also discuss the completed playdates per the booking and control form. He is to be 'on top' of these playdates and always pushing for new ones.

PUBLIC CONTACT

It is the natural osmosis of a distribution company to grow. No company remains in a constant state. The company grows bigger or smaller. The only way a motion picture distribution company grows is by obtaining an increase of motion pictures for distribution. The sales manager should always be aware of this. He should exert great efforts toward acquiring new products. These new products are only obtained through motion picture producers who are seeking an alert and ambitious distribution company. He knows that a company of this calibre will do their utmost to earn the highest possible income on his film. Both parties gain and a relationship may develop where the distributor and the producer work together on new projects and developments.

To acquire this new product the sales manager must seek new films every day. This is accomplished through media advertising and more effectively through word of mouth. Additionally, the sales manager should study the production charts listed in motion picture periodicals and contact the producers who are in production prior to completion. The producer will be impressed with the aggressiveness of the distribution company and will, in all probability, contact the distribution company after completion of the film for the possible distribution of his film.

The sales manager must be active in advising those working on pressbooks, one sheets and the all-important motion picture trailer. He should also keep up with trends and have a total grasp of the market requirements and tastes. This can only be obtained through extensive research and public contact. Theatres and exchanges are invaluable for helping to obtain this information. Group meetings with other distribution companies and organizations are also helpful. He must be active with the public.

Occasionally, the sales manager must work independently of the exchange. He must book his own films. The procedure is identical with an exchange booking except that direct contact is made with the theatre by the sales manager. Terms and conditions are negotiated by the sales manager and the theatre rather than by an exchange. These types of bookings are called *house accounts*.

HOUSE ACCOUNTS

When a distribution company books directly, there is no commission for the exchange. The distribution makes the sales contract and ships the motion picture directly to the theatre. Almost always, the booking is on a percentage date with a sliding scale and guarantees. Advertising budgets are discussed and approved by both parties. Then a playdate is set.

When both the sales manager and the theatre are satisfied with all arrangements, the sales manager makes up a theatre booking contract (Fig. 11-1). All theatre contracts are basically the same.

When the contract is made it is handled as a booking and the booking and control clerk will enter the booking on the booking and control sheet. All procedures will then be the same as if the exchange made the booking.

This booking form (Fig. 11-1) is for house accounts. It lists the following information:

Exchange: List the state and the location of the exchange area, i.e. Los Angeles, New York, etc.

Date: This is the date of the contract.

Salesman: In this case it would be the sales manager making the direct sale.

Theatre: List the name of the theatre.

Town and state: List the address of the theatre.

Picture: List the name of the motion picture.

Run: List the playdates.

Rental: List the terms of sales, i.e. percentage date, or flat or other conditions relative to the playdate.

Advertising: List the advertising budget agreed to before the booking and all conditions agreed upon in advertising. Also if advertising is to be shared, list what percentage of sharing.

cricket film
productions inc.

3516 CAHUENGA WEST
HOLLYWOOD, CA. 90038
(213) 876-6255

EXCHANGE _____ DATE _____ SALESMAN _____

THEATRE		TOWN AND STATE
PICTURES:		
RUN:		
RENTAL:		
ADVERTISING		

ADDITIONAL PROVISIONS

142

MAILING ADDRESS

RUN

CLEARANCE

NOTICE: Shipment will not be made unless approved co-op advertising agreement is received by us two (2) weeks prior to playdate. We do not share in trailer, accessories, lobby display or ticket expenditures.

ALL SUMS PAID AS A CONDITION OF ADMISSION SHALL BE INCLUDED IN 'GROSS RECEIPTS FOR THE PURPOSE OF DETERMINING FILM RENTAL

NOTICE TO EXHIBITOR:—If two or more features are included in this contract, it is simply for convenience and this application is a separate application for each picture. The rules of this Company require that each feature should be separately offered to you, the contract therefore separately negotiated, and that the rental of any picture should not be conditioned upon the rental of another.

IN WITNESS WHEREOF, the Parties hereto have duly executed these presents including the provisions on the back of this page.

DATE

EXHIBITOR

BY

GENERAL SALES MGR.

SIGNATORY

Fig. 11-1. A sample theatre booking contract.

Additional provisions: Any pertinent information about the playdate should be recorded in this space.

Mailing address: If the mailing address of theatre is other than that stated in theatre address, then so indicate.

Signatures: Both the exhibitor and the general sales manager should sign this agreement indicating the playdate. The contract should be dated to make this a legal contract.

All other conditions will be considered as a normal booking. The booking and control clerk will be responsible for getting the print to the theatre two days prior to the actual playdate.

RUNS

It is the responsibility of the distributor to obtain maximum income from the distribution of the Producer's film. The method of exposure of the film is vitally important. As stated previously, most of this responsibility rests on the shoulders of the sales manager. If the distributor has a good commercial picture he can use several distribution formulas.

First Run

The distributor opens the film in a large city in a one-theatre break, maximum advertising and press is devoted to this opening break. Many times, the distributor is lucky to break even on this one theatre break due to the cost of the expended advertising and publicity. If the picture holds for several weeks, this cost can be amortized and eventually a substantial profit can be realized.

However, the intent of a *first run* premium playdate is to advertise the picture and create the feeling that this is a big important picture. It is initially a set-up for the more normal distribution.

Second Run

This run is a normal means of distribution with multiple theatres participating in the release of the film. They all share the cost of advertising. Many times in a large city such as New York, as many as 50 theatres maybe showing the film in the same week. The picture runs *top of the bill*. The other picture has already played these areas and they receive a *flat price*. The distributor pays this flat price out of revenue received from the multiple. Since the cost of advertising is amortized over many theatres, this will, in many cases, be the largest income-producing playdate for the film.

Sub-Run

This run follows the second multiple run. It is made on the heels of the second run and takes advantage of the previous publicity and exposure received by the picture so far. This *sub-run* includes pick-up theatres not necessarily included in the multiple. However, it can very well include some of the second run theatres if they so desire. The advertising, of course, is much lower since the public is aware of the name of the picture and the contents of the previous ads. Smaller ads are used in this sub-run. The income will probably be less than the second run but since the cost of advertising is also lower, it can still result in as much net profit to the distributor.

Combo-Run

At this point, a combo-run can be effective. This is when two pictures of similar content will run together as a double-bill. Hopefully, this will be a second run and both films will share the top-of-the-bill. The theatre pays a percentage to the distributor, i.e. 25 percent, and each film is allocated 12-1/2 percent of the income. This can be particularly beneficial with horror films, science fiction, etc. Occasionally, three films can fit into this combo-run. Of course, then the income is split 33-1/3 percent each.

Flat Run

Finally, the distributor books the film flat. This means that the distributor pays the producer a flat price for the film. These flat prices are very low but since the film has exhausted the market, it is virtually extra money for the producer. This type of flat run is usually teamed with the second run of a new film coming out. *Flat runs* are priced weekly and if the new film has any hold over powers, then each week the distributor would receive from the exhibitor another week's flat run price. The top picture *percentage run* pays for this out of its income.

FOUR WALL DISTRIBUTION

Four wall distribution is another means of booking a film. This is open to the conditions existing at the time of the playdate.

The meaning of the term four walls literally means, renting the full theatre which includes four walls. It is a complete rental. The rental is for the period of time agreed upon between the theatre and the distributor.

DATE	RENTAL DATES			OPTIONAL RENTAL DATES			CONTRACT NO.
	From	To	Total Rent	From	To	Option Rent	

T.V. AREA
THE
THEATRE   PHONE NO.

CITY.
COUNTY
STATE
COUNTRY
    ADMISSION ADULTS   JR.
    CHILDREN 12 AND UNDER
    SEATING CAPACITY
    AFFILIATION

This agreement is made and entered into between _____ (hereinafter referred to as Exhibitor) and theatre owner or operator identified below (hereinafter referred to as Owner).
Exhibitor has a "G" Rated Motion Picture Film for Exhibition to the public for admission and the Owner has facilities suitable to show such a motion picture film or films to the public for admission.
Now, THEREFORE, it is hereby agreed as follows:

1. Owner hereby agrees that said film will be exhibited in the Theatre under the terms and conditions herein specified and in consideration agrees to maintain the Theatre in which the film is shown fully staffed with necessary projectionists, ticket sellers and ticket takers. Exhibitor agrees to provide prints for such showings.

2. Owner agrees that for a period of 45 days prior to the first rental date set forth above, it will not show in the Theatre in which the above-specified film is to be shown or in any other theatre owned, managed or under the control of Owner which is located in the television advertising market in which the Theatre is located, as defined in "T.V. Fact Book", any "G" rated film which is similar in nature as the above-specified film, uses a similar method of sales approach as the above-specified film or the advertising for which utilizes extensive T.V. saturation advertising.

3. Owner agrees to conduct showings of the film under the supervision of a duly appointed representative of Exhibitor and further agrees to return this film, free of undue wear and tear, immediately following the last performance at which the film is shown.

4. Owner agrees to furnish box office change.

5. Owner agrees to display one sheets and run trailers provided by the National Screen Service or Exhibitor and display the marquee in the customary manner.

6. Owner agrees to assist Exhibitor in obtaining local rates for local newspaper and radio advertising; Exhibitor agrees to pay for all advertising authorized in writing by its representative.
7. All tickets will be furnished by Exhibitor.
8. Exhibitor reserves the right at all showings to secure samplings of audience reaction by means of questionnaires, and to sell brochures or other items relating to the film or any other films which it may possess.
9. Owner agrees to open the box office 30 minutes prior to each show.
10. Owner agrees to issue no passes or discounts for admission to any performance of the film and agrees to honor any such passes or discounts which Exhibitor may from time to time issue.
11. Owner agrees that immediately following each showing of the above-specified film, it will pay Exhibitor, in cash, the exact amount of ticket sales revenue from such showing (Overages or Shortages will not be accepted). Out of the gross receipts for each showing of the above-specified film, Exhibitor agrees to pay Owner an amount equal to all admission taxes for tickets sold for said showing and Owner agrees to pay said sum to the proper governmental agency and to furnish Exhibitor with a tax receipt evidencing payment of said sum to the proper governmental agency and a statement signed by Owner setting forth the amount of tax withheld per ticket, total tickets sold for said showing and total tax withheld for said showing.
12. In the event that the Theatre is destroyed, or is damaged so as to render it wholly or partially unusable, prior to completion of the showing hereunder, at the toption of Exhibitor, this agreement will be terminated.
13. Owner hereby agrees to show the film at all of the following times:

                No. Shows (Last show to start no later than 9:00 P.M.)

    Weekdays—
    Saturdays—
    Sundays—

14. As full consideration for compliance with all of the terms and conditions specified herein, the owner shall receive the sum of
15. The agreement shall be deemed to have been entered into and shall be governed by the laws of the state in which the theatre is located.

    Payment To:
                            Theatre Manager:
    Terms of Payment: Name
                            Phone No. (   )
    Comments:

    EXECUTED the   Day of   ,19

By: _____   _____
    "Theatre Owner" (signature)   "Exhibitor" (Film Owner)   Empl. No.

Fig. 11-2. A typical four wall contract for a film exhibition.

In this type of arrangement, the distributor takes all risks, paying for all promotional and advertising costs and guaranteeing the theatre a flat rental for the period of theatre rental.

Four wall booking is usually reserved for the independent distributor. It can be very lucrative but it can also be very risky. It requires extensive promotion including advertising on the local television station. It should also be supported with a print campaign. Also it is essential to have market research available including audience reactions and trends.

The distributor via his sales manager, must possess excellent, specialized marketing and demographic skills. Also he must be aware of competing films and sport events which could cut heavily into his advertising campaign.

Occasionally, the distributor might want to spread the risk. In that case he would make a deal with a theatre. The theatre might share in the overage income of the distributor after the distributor makes an agreed-upon gross income from the exhibition of the motion picture. This would, of course, be for a cheaper theatre rental.

The advantages of the four wall principle is that the distributor controls the advertising. He also has total supervision over all box office receipts at the end of each night's playdate.

This type of distribution should only be considered if the sales manager has an excellent film and he feels the demand for this type of film is strong enough. For four wall bookings, the sales manager books direct and issues the four wall contract (Fig. 11-2).

Notice that this type of contract is much more specific than the normal percentage or flat rental contract. It limits the theatre's control of the playdate time and binds the theatre into a mandatory number of showings. It also states the theatre rental charges and virtually puts the control of the theatre into the hands of the distributor.

A breakdown of this contract is as follows:

Date: List the date of the contract.

Rental dates: List the rental period plus the total rent for that period.

Optional rent: In the case of a holdover, the theatre options to hold the preceeding film for a longer Period. The optional rent dates would be listed in this space.

Contract No.: List the contract number (made by distributor).

T.V. Area: List the code for the TV area.

Theatre: List the name of the theatre.

Address: List the total address of the theatre including country.

Prices: List the agreed upon admission prices of tickets.

Seating: List the number of seats in the theatre.

Affiliation: List the circuit (if any) of the theatre.

Terms: Insert the name of the distributor (hereinafter referred to as exhibitor).

No. Shows: List the number of shows per day plus the time of each showing.

Payment: List the rental agreed upon for the theatre date.

Payment to: List the name and address of the theatre.

Theatre Mgr: List the name of the manager of the theatre or alternate.

Phone No.: List the number where the manager can be reached at all times.

Signatures: Both the sales manager of the distribution company and the authorized manager of the theatre should sign and date the form.

In all cases, including direct theatre booking on percentages, flat rentals and wall-to-walll bookings, the sales manager will advise the booking and control clerk.

For his internal control of all bookings, the sales manager will file his completed copy of the booking and control sheet under following filing system:

■ The filing will be first by state.

■ Under the state it will then be filed by city.

■ Under the city, it will be filed in alphabetical order by theatres.

All bookings will be a permanent record and will correspond with the recapitulation of cut-off playdates form (exhibitor's record cards) which the sales manager receives from the accounts receivable department. It is simple to check these playdates when the filing system just described is used.

BOX OFFICE AND ADMISSIONS CHECK

At times it is advisable to check the theatre admissions. Usually this is impossible for the distributor to do if the theatre is located far from their offices. In most cases, it is advisable to hire a professional agency who specializes in theatre testing and theatre ticket sales. They are expensive but if the distributor feels that the expense warrants the control, then it is worth it.

Most agencies charge a flat fee for each test plus automobile or travel expenses. The contract is based on the number of tests

INVOICE

UNIFORMED GUARDS
APPLICANT INVESTIGATIONS
SECURITY SURVEYS & PLANNING
SURVEILLANCES & INVESTIGATIONS
ELECTRONIC PROTECTIVE DEVICES

417 SOUTH HILL STREET
LOS ANGELES, CALIFORNIA 90013

OFFICES IN PRINCIPAL CITIES IN
UNITED STATES AND CANADA
MEMBER OF THE LIGUE
INTERNATIONALE DES SOCIETIES
DE SURVEILLANCE

INVOICE NUMBER _____

JOURNAL NUMBER _____
5/20/
INVOICE DATE _____

TO: CRICKET FILM PROD. INC.

TERMS: NET—PAYABLE UPON RECEIPT OF INVOICE

FOR SERVICES RENDERED RE: TESTING—THEATER TICKET SELLERS

AWM	5/3, 10/75	4 TEST @	15.00	$60.00	
EXPENSES			12.60 AUTO	27.60	$87.60
JAJ	5/2/75	2 TEST @	15.00	$30.00	
EXPENSES			15.10	21.10	51.10
		TOTAL			$138.70

TOTAL: _____ $138.70
PREVIOUS BALANCE: _____
GRAND TOTAL: _____

PLEASE RETURN TRIPLICATE COPY WITH YOUR REMITTANCE

Fig. 11-3. A sample invoice from a professional agency specializing in theatre testing.

required, i.e. daily or periodical testing (every other day). Figure 11-3 illustrates an invoice from such an agency. The office procedures and accounting for control of the distribution of the motion picture might seem complicated, but they are in reality, quite simple. If the breakdown is made step-by-step it unfolds itself and clarifies the progressive nature of the system. Everything has an order. To maintain complete control, one must follow that order.

Chapter 12

The Television Market

Television sales are usually made after a motion picture has been in theatrical distribution for more than two years. Sales can be made in advance of that time period but television exhibition usually starts after the two-year exposure. There are basically two types of television sales: network sales and syndication sales.

NETWORK SALES

If the motion picture has excellent production values and has a "big name" cast, networks are interested in playing the film on national television in prime time slots (usually 8 to 11 p.m.). Networks, meaning, ABC, CBS and NBC, consists of five O & O's (owned and operated) plus numerous affiliated stations which comprise the network group. The Federal Communications Commission only allows a group to own five stations in the U.S.A. There are many independent groups such as Westinghouse Broadcasting, Metromedia, Storer Broadcasting, etc. who also own five stations. These companies are a quasi-type of mini networks.

Sale to a network is negotiated. The price depends on the cast and how well the film did in theatrical distribution. Network sales are for two runs. The first run (first time on television) is usually exhibited in the prime season-September through June. The re-runs are during the summer months of July through August when the viewing audience is down due to vacations and other summer activities.

If a network is interested in showing the motion picture, they will pay the distributor a price ranging from $500,000.00 to $750,000.00, again depending on the drawing power of the film. In the case of block-busting films, the price range runs into the millions of dollars for two showings.

Most of the motion pictures shown on national television are supplied by the major distribution companies, such as Universal-International, Columbia Pictures, Paramount, etc.

These major distributors also work closely with the networks on *Movies of the Week* and films made explicitly for television viewing. The major distributors usually reserve foreign rights and these films are distributed as full length motion pictures on the international market. Many times, the major distributor realizes profits from the international market and is content to recoup the production costs from television.

It is apparent that a small independent distributor cannot compete too well in the network market. First of all, his feature motion pictures usually will be budgeted at a low cost with no real value. This type of film does not interest the networks. Secondly, networks prefer to work with the large motion picture distributors since they require large blocks of films. They also know that most of the major films are receptive to the television viewing audience.

Occasionally, a low budgeted film has an overwhelming appeal and does very well at the box office. If it wins awards and national recognition, it stands a chance of getting on national television. However, these cases are very rare.

Tha natural sequence for the independent motion picture distributor is to seek other avenues of television distribution. This avenue falls into the category of syndication sales.

SYNDICATION SALES

There are literally hundreds of television stations throughout the United States that do not get the chance to purchase network products. The price may be too high or the previous exposure of re-runs makes it undesirable for them to show the product.

Many independent television stations like to group films in a like category, such as horror or science-fiction shows. They can compete with network shows because they are assured of receiving show buffs. These same buffs would not view the old standard classics of horror and science-fiction. In fact, these types of films are very lucrative to the independent TV market and commands the most revenue.

It is extremely difficult for an independent motion picture distributor to enter the market of TV syndication since most stations want to purchase films in blocks of 13. The TV syndicator has access to many independent distributors and he makes TV distribution arrangements with them on an individual basis. Then he accumulates the minimum requirements of thirteen and sells those films as a block sale.

There are two types of television syndication sales: outright sale to TV station and percentage engagements to TV station.

Outright Sale to TV Station

These sales are made outright in perpetuity (forever). It gives the television station unlimited runs of the motion picture and becomes a library item in their stable of films. The television station can show the series of films, hold them back for several years and then run the films again and again. These sales are made for a flat fee. Additionally, the sale can be made while the film is still in theatrical distribution. Monies can be advanced up to 24 months before the television station actually receives the film rights for television. These sales are all final.

Percentage Engagements to TV station

These sales are made on a percentage engagement and negotiated by the television distributor. The stations pay a fee for the series and then they continue to pay per each re-run.

In these cases, the motion picture television rights always belong to the motion picture distributor and the producer.

All motion pictures made after 1960 must have the provisions (if made with the screen actors' guild) that the artists will receive residual payments each time the motion picture is projected on television. However, these payments are only for a certain number of exposures. The common number is eight re-runs.

If a motion picture is made using all union personnel, then the producer can buy-out the residual rights. This is in accordance with union regulations and procedures and should be thoroughly investigated.

Occasionally, a network (or the five owned and operated stations), may elect to run a syndicated series not in prime time (time other than 8 p.m. to 11 p.m.). These sales are considered as syndication sales and not network sales.

In view of the highly specialized market in television sales, it is strongly suggested that the motion picture distributor employ the services of a television distributor to sell motion pictures. There are many reasons for this. One reason is that the motion picture distributor must have a minimum of 13 motion pictures in the same category and of the same degree of motion picture ratings. You cannot play a G film with several R rates films. A second reason is that the motion picture distributor must staff competent personnel who specialize in television sales.

Unless the motion picture distribution firm is very large, it cannot affect sales. Subsequently, most independents use the services of the *TV distribution company*. In line with this, a typical *television distribution contract* is found in Fig. 12-1. The term *distributor* in this case refers to the television distributor and the term *owner* refers to the distribution company or producer.

TV distribution contracts usually run seven years with renewal clauses unless the motion picture distributor or producer advises the television distributor to the contrary.

In this agreement the following items are adhered to:

■ Length and term of the contract.

■ Name of the distributor and/or producer and television distributor.

■ Name of motion picture.

■ Percentage of distribution of income and disbursement of gross receipts.

■ The date of signing the agreement and necessary signatures.

The television distributor either contacts the television stations directly or through his own sub-distributors. They will negotiate all television sales and receive a percentage of the gross receipts from a sale.

All income received by the distributor shall be in accordance with procedures outlined previously such as the booking and control clerk; the accounts receivable department; the sales manager; and the master control unit.

The booking and control clerk will be responsible again for advising all of these departments as to income received and for keeping track of all prints. He will also assist the television distributor on all necessary items pertaining to the distribution of the motion picture.

Figure 12-2 is a sample of a television sales contract sent to a television station. Notice in the *Contract of License* (No. 7 - clearance) that no license can be granted to any other television stations within a radius of 40 miles of each station until the total series has been telecast.

TELEVISION DISTRIBUTION AGREEMENT

In consideration of their reciprocal agreements hereinafter set forth, _____, a _____ Corporation, hereinafter referred to as "Distributor," and _____ hereinafter referred to as "Owner," agree as follows:

1. **Distribution Rights.** Owner hereby grants and assigns to Distributor the sole and exclusive right to distribute, exhibit, exploit, televise and market, or cause to be exhibited, the photoplay or photoplays set forth in Exhibit "A" attached hereto and made a part hereof (hereinafter referred to collectively and individually as the "photoplay") throughout the licensed territory, for a period of ___ years, commencing _____ (hereinafter referred to as the "original term"). For the purpose of this agreement, the licensed territory is hereby defined as _____ provided, however, that if there remain outstanding on the date of the termination of thsi agreement any contracts for the exhibition of he photoplay, such contracts shall remain in full force and effect until their expiration and may continue to be performed by Distributor or its licensees, but for no more than ___ years after the date of suck termination. Without limiting the generality of any of the provisions of this agreement in which reference is made to the rights granted to Distributor or in which such rights are described, it is agreed that the rights so granted shall include:

(a) The right (but not the obligation) to cut, edit and otherwise alter and adapt the photoplay for television use for the purpose of meeting time and sponsorship considerations;

(b) The right to insert commercial, advertising and exploitation matter or materials of such nature therein;

(c) The right to make changes in the photoplay for the purposes of foreign distribution, including but not limited to superimposed and dubbed versions; and

(d) The right to permit, authorize and license others to exercise and enjoy all or any of Distributor's rights and licenses hereunder, in accordance with the provisions of this agreement.

The phrases "television" or "television use" as used herein shall be deemed to include, but shall not be limited to, the transmission, projection or exhibition of visual (with or without audible sounds) performances over the air or by wire by any means now or hereafter known or conceived to non-paying audiences or viewers located at homes, studios, theatres, arenas, auditoriums, stadiums, or any other places now or hereafter known or used, and shall also include, without limitation, the transmission, projection, or exhibition of television photoplays, or the audible part thereof, whether or not separated from said television photoplays, by radio means, television means, or both.

Further, in the event licenses of exhibition are granted by distributor outside of the continental United States, as defined in paragraph one, it is considered common industry practice to supply licensee additional printa for sub-standard non-theatrical exhibition by means of normal 16 mm projection. The primary purpose is to reach small segments of audiences unable to receive the primary television signal in a given territory. Such additional extended usage shall be deemed included herein.

2. **Owner's Warranties.** Owner represents and warrants that it has the full right, power and authority to enter into this agreement and to grant all of the rights herein granted and/or agreed to be granted; that it owns the complete and exclusive distribution, performance, exhibition and reproduction rights in any and all media in and to the photoplay, together with the right to use in publicizing, advertising and exploiting the same, the names, characters and text thereof; that the recordings of music and sound from any part of such photoplay shall be duly authorized by the owners of the rights of such recordings, and that it has the full and unencumbered mechanical recording, copying, reproducing and performing rights throughout the licensed territory of all dialogue and material (including music) included in the sound recorded in synchronization with the photoplay; that nothing contained in the photoplay will be grounds for action to prevent the exhibition thereof on television or otherwise or for damages in connection therewith by reason of the fact that it is slanderous or libelous, and invasion of any right of privacy, a violation of any copyright or other personal or property rights or for any other reason whatsoever, and that Owner will indemnify Distributor and hold it harmless from and against any loss, liability, damage, settlement, judgement, expenses and costs, including attorneys' fees, suffered, made, incurred or assumed by Distributor resulting from any breach or alleged breach of any warranties, representations or covenants made by Owner in this agreement; and that the photoplay is now ready in all respects for distribution.

3. **Delivery.** Owner, at its own cost and expense, shall deliver to Distributor, at a laboratory of Distributor's choice, all necessary negatives, fine grains, masters, dialogue and sound track, music and effects track and positive prints of the photoplay as requested by Distributor, in 16 mm or 35 mm width and in balck and white or color.

4. **Gross Receipts.** The term "gross receipts" as used in this agreement shall be deemed to be all monies actually paid to and received by Distributor in dollars in the United States, or in other currency freely remittable to the United States, as rental or license fees to exhibit and televise the photoplay; provided that advance payments or security deposits shall not be included until or unless the same have been earned or forfeited, and amounts collected by Distributor for taxes or for payment of taxes shall not be included therein. No warranty or representation is made by Distributor as to the amount of gross receipts which may be derived from the distribution of the photoplay, and Owner agrees to make no claim or assert any liability against Distributor on the ground that better prices or terms should or could have been obtained by Distributor, so long as Distributor's judgement is exercised in good faith. If the photoplay is licensed for sub-distribution or exhibition under any agreement which licenses the distribution or exhibition, as the case may be, of one or more motion pictures, but which does not specify the license fee, rental or sales price of the photoplay, the allocation of the amount to be deemed attributable to the photoplay shall be determined by Distributor in its sole discretion, and such determination shall be binding and conclusive upon Owner.

Fig. 12-1. A typical television distribution contract.

5. **Disbursement of Gross Receipts.** Prior to any disbursement of gross receipts, Distributor shall be entitled to recoup and retain: (a) An amount equal to the cost of all alboratory components required and release prints for the photoplay, together with any and all shipping charges as may not have been prepaid by Owner; and (b) All costs of advertising, exploitation and publicity; provided, however, that no more than $_____ may be incurred for such costs in any consecutive 12 month period without the prior written consent of Owner. From the remaining gross receipts, Distributor shall recoup and retain __% as its distribution fee from proceeds within the United States and the Dominion of Canada, and shall pay to Owner __% of such gross receipts. The proceeds from all other territories as defined in paragraph one shall be on a fifty/fifty basis after the recoupments as herein provided.

6. **Distribution Records.** Distributor agrees to keep true, accurate and complete books of account with respect to the distribution of the photoplay showing gross receipts. Such books of account and records shall be kept by Distributor at such place or places as may from time to time be customary for Distributor in accordance with Distributor's ordinary business practices. Owner shall have the right, at Owner's sole cost and expense, to inspect, audit and make extracts from such books and records, but with respect only to the photoplay, at reasonable times during business hours, but not more often than once during each calendar quarter. No claim by Owner that any charge, computation or deduction shown or reflected in any statement rendered to Owner by Distributor is improper or inaccurate shall be asserted by Owner or any successor or assign of Owner unless made in writing to Distributor within one (1) year after the date of each such statement containing such item is rendered.

7. **Statements and Payments.** As soon as practicable, and no later than thirty days following each of its accounting periods (of which there shall be a minimum of __ each year) and commencing with the accounting period in which collections are first received by Distributor with respect to the photoplay, Distributor shall deliver to Owner a statement of the gross receipts of the photoplay and of the deductions therefrom, and any amounts shown in any such statement to be payable, as provided in paragraph five hereof, shall be paid concurrently with the rendition of such statement.

8. **Force Majeure.** Neither Owner nor Distributor shall be liable to the other in damages because of failure or delay in performance due to fire, earthquake, flood, epidemic, accident, explosion, casualty, strike, lockout, labor controversy, unavoidable accident, riot, civil disturbance, act of public enemy, embargo, war, act of God, any muncipal, state or federal ordinance or law, any order, regulation or decree of any judicial or other legally constituted authority, whether municipal, state or federal, failure or delay of any transportation agency, failure or delay caused by any equipment or apparatus or of any laboratory, failure without fault to obtain materials, trnasportation, power or any other essential thing required in its business, or by any other causes reasonably beyond the control of such party. In the event that any such contingency shall continue for a period or aggregate of periods in excess of ninety (90) days either party hereto shall have the right to terminate this agreement.

9. Option. In consideration of the covenants and agreements herein contained, Owner hereby grants to Distributor options to distribute the photoplay, during one or more successive periods of one (1) year each, commencing upon the expiration of the original term (each such period is hereinafter referred to as the "optional period"). Each such option shall be automatically exercised unless Distributor or Owner shall render written notice to the other that it does not desire said renewed at least sixty (60) days prior to the expiration of the original term or the then current optional period, as the case may be; provided, however, that Owner shall have the right to terminate this agreement, but only during an optional period as of the date of expiration of the then current optional period, by notice to Distributor at least sixty (60) days prior to the expiration thereof.

10. **Agency.** Nothing contained in this agreement shall constitute a partnership between or joint venture by the parties hereto, or constitute either party the agent of the other. Neither of the parties hereto shall hold itself out contrary to the terms of this paragraph, and neither of the parties shall become liable by the representation, act or omission of the other contrary to the provisions hereof.

11. **Notices.** All notices hereunder or in connection herewith and all statements shall be addressed as follows:
To Distributor: _____ or at such other address as from time to time the respective parties may designate in writing. Such notices shall be served and statements rendered by depositing them addressed as aforesaid, postage prepaid, in the United States mail, or by delivering them, charges prepaid, to a telegraph company. Any notices served by mail shall be registered or certified, with return receipt requested. The date of mailing of any notice or the date of delivery thereof to the telegraph company shall constitute the date of service. Payments to Owner may also be made by regular mail addressed as aforesaid.

12. **Termination.** Upon the expiration of the term of this agreement all physical properties relating to the photoplay then in the possession of Distributor shall be returned to Owner at Owner's sole cost and expense.

13. **Miscellaneous.** The captions of the various paragraphs of this agreement are intended solely for convenience of reference and shall not be deemed to amend or aid in the construction of any of the provisions of this agreement.
Throughout this agreement the singular shall include the plural, and the plural shall include the singular.
The use herein of the neuter pronoun shall be deemed to include any individual, corporation or co-partnership, as the context of the sentence where used may reasonably require.

IN WITNESS WHEREOF, the parties hereto have executed this agreement this _____ day of _____, 19 at _____.

By _____

Its _____

Distributor _____

Fig. 12-1. A typical television distribution contract (continued from page 158).

THE FOLLOWING SCHEDULE AND ALL OF THE **WRITTEN** AND **PRINTED** PARTS THEREOF ARE A PART OF THIS LICENSE AGREEMENT:

STATION	CITY	STATE	DATE	CONTRACT NO.

SCHEDULE A

TITLE OF PICTURE	DATE OF TELECAST	NO. OF PERFORMANCES	HUNNING TIME	FILM WIDTH	LICENSE FEE	
					SUSTAINING	SPONSERED.

SCHEDULE B

NOTICES—THE ADDRESSES OF THE PARTIES HERETO FOR THE PURPOSE OF SERVICE OF NOTICES AND MAKING PAYMENTS ARE THE FOLLOWING:

DISTRIBUTOR—
LICENSEE—

IN WITNESS WHEREOF, LICENSEE HAS ON THIS _____ DAY OF _____ , 19 ____ , EXCUTED THIS APPLICATION, WHICH UPON ACCEPTANCE IN WRITING BY DISTRIBUTOR AT ITS HOME OFFICE IN HOLLYWOOD, CALIF., SHALL CONSTITUTE A CONTRACT OF LICENSE FOR THE TELECAST OF THE PICTURE HEREIN IN ACCORDANCE WITH THE TERMS AND CONDITIONS HEREOF.

BY _____
"DISTRIBUTOR"

BY _____
"LICENSE"

Fig. 12-2. A sample television sales contract.

Dated: _____

Agreement between QUBE, a division of Warner Cable Corp., 75 Rockefeller Plaza, New York, New York 10019 ("QUBE") and ART GREENFIELD CO., 9255 Sunset Bouelvard, Suite 901, Los Angeles, California 90069 ("Licensor").

WITNESSETH:

1. Licensor hereby grants and assigns to QUBE the right under copyright to exhibit, exploit, transmit, project and perform the programs described in Exhibit "A" annexed hereto (the "Programs") on QUBE's pay television system located in Columbus, Ohio. The rights granted to QUBE hereunder shall include:

(a) the right, subject to paragraph four, to use and perform any and all music lyrics and musical compositions contained in the Programs.

(b) the right to make such cuts and eliminations in the Programs as QUBE may require in order to meet time segment requirements, censorship requirements or otherwise to adapt and make the Programs suitable for exhibition hereunder, provided that neither the copyright notice nor the credits appearing on the main or end titles of the Programs shall be cut or eliminated;

(c) the right, for the purpose of advertising, publicizing and exploiting the Programs, to publish synopses, excerpts and summaries of not more than 3,000 words in length from the Programs;

(d) to use such advertising and publicity materials as Licensor shall make available, it being understood that Licensor shall make available to QUBE such materials as shall be available to Licensor and requested by QUBE;

(e) the right to advertise, publicize and promote the exhibition of the Programs by any means or media, except that QUBE shall not, for such purpose, utilize excerpts of more than five (5) minutes in length from each of the Programs.

2. The duration of this agreement shall be a period of two (2) years commencing on the date of first broadcast of the Programs hereunder or January 1, 1978, whichever shall be earlier. During the duration of this agreement, QUBE shall have the right to exhibit the Programs for such number of exhibitions as QUBE shall determine.

162

3. Licensor agrees to deliver the Programs to QUBE by delivering to QUBE, at such laboratory as QUBE shall designate (the "Laboratory"), within ten (10) days following receipt of QUBE's written request therefor, which request may be made by QUBE at any time following the execution of this agreement, a first-class thirty five (35 mm) millimeter or, if unavailable, a sixteen (16 mm) millimeter color positive print (or duplicate videotape) of each of the Programs suitable for transfer or conversion to broadcast quality videotape. All transportation charges for redelivery of such prints or videotapes to Licensor shall be borne by QUBE.

Title to all positive prints or videotapes delivered by Licensor to the Laboratory shall at all times remain the property of Licensor and shall be returned to Licensor within thirty (30) days following receipt by the Laboratory.

Within seven (7) days of the expiration of the duration of this agreement, QUBE shall degause or destroy all videotapes and cassettes made of the Programs. At the request of Licensor, QUBE shall, after degausing or destroying such videotapes or cassettes, provide to Licensor certificates of degausing or destruction with respect to the videotapes and cassettes of the Programs.

QUBE shall employ reasonable security measures to prevent the loss, theft or unauthorized duplication of any of the Program videotapes, cassettes or prints created by or in the possession of QUBE.

4. Licensor warrants and represents to QUBE that the performance rights to all musical compositions contained in the Programs are (i) controlled by the American Society of Composers, Authors and Publishers (ASCAP), Broadcast Music Inc. (BMI) or SESAC; (ii) in the public domain; or (iii) controlled by Licensor to the extent required for the purpose of this agreement. Except for such performance rights as are controlled by Licensor, it shall be QUBE's responsibility to obtain all necessary licenses for the performance of the musical compositions contained in the Programs.

5. Licensor warrants and represents to QUBE that the Programs, when delivered, will be completely finished, fully edited and titled and fully synchronized with language, dialogue, sound and music (if any); that Licensor has the absolute right to grant to QUBE all of the rights granted to QUBE hereunder; that the rights herein granted are free and clear of any liens or claims whatsoever in favor of any party whomsoever; and that the use of the Programs as herein provided will not violate or infringe any copyright or constitute a libel or defamation of, or invasion of the rights of privacy or publicity of any party; that all claims scripts,

Fig. 12-3. A copy of a pay television agreement between a pay station and a producer.

themes, incidents, plots, characters, dialogue, music, words and other material of any nature appearing, use or recorded in the Programs and all claims and rights with respect to the use, distribution, performance and exhibition of the Programs and any music contained therein on QUBE's pay television system have been fully paid and discharged; and that no payments shall be payable to any union or guild by reason of, or as a condition for, any use, re-use or re-run of the Programs on QUBE's pay television system.

Licensor hereby agrees to indemnify and hold QUBE harmless against any claims, demands, or causes of action arising out of the breach of any of the foregoing warranties or representations. Upon notice from QUBE of any such claim, demand or action being advanced or commenced, Licensor agrees to adjust, settle or defend the same at the sole cost of Licensor; if Licensor shall fail promptly so to do, QUBE shall have the right and is hereby authorized and empowered by Licensor to appear by its attorneys in any such action, to adjust, settle, compromise, litigate, contest, satisfy judgments and take any other action necessary or desirable for the disposition of such claim, demand or action; in any such case Licensor, within fifteen (15) days after demand therefore by QUBE, shall fully reimburse QUBE for all such payments and expenses, including attorneys' fees.

6. In full consideration of the rights granted to QUBE hereunder and in consideration of Licensor's warranties and representations, QUBE shall pay to Licensor an amount equal to twenty (20%) percent of the gross receipts derived by QUBE from the exhibition of the Programs hereunder, which sums shall be computed and paid as provided in Exhibit "1" annexed hereto and made a part hereof.

7. This agreement constitutes the entire agreement between the parties. This agreement may not be changed, altered or modified except by written instrument duly executed by each of the parties hereto, and this provision may not be waived except by an instrument in writing signed by each of the parties.

IN WITNESS WHEREOF, the parties hereto have duly executed this agreement the day above written.

QUBE, a division of
WARNER CABLE CORP.

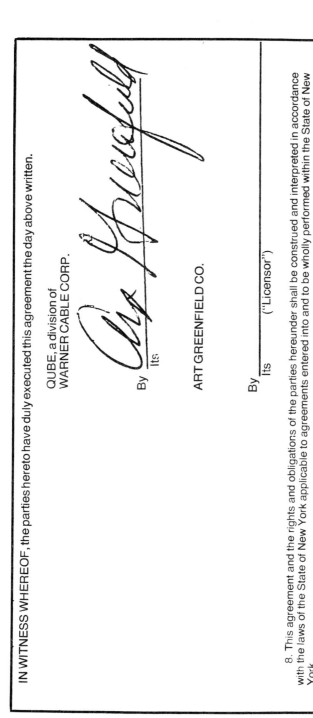

By _____
Its:

ART GREENFIELD CO.

By _____
Its   ("Licensor")

8. This agreement and the rights and obligations of the parties hereunder shall be construed and interpreted in accordance with the laws of the State of New York applicable to agreements entered into and to be wholly performed within the State of New York.

Fig. 12-3. A copy of pay television agreement between a pay station and a producer (continued from page 164).

ART GREENFIELD COMPANY
9255 SUNSET BOULEVARD
LOS ANGELES, CA. 90069

(SUITE 507)
TEL: (213) 273-0418

Date_____

DISTRIBUTION AGREEMENT

address_____

Dear:

It has been mutually agreed between us that the Art Greenfield Company, shall become your—distributor for the pictures_____, for television and ancillary television areas with the following terms and conditions to prevail:

1. Art Greenfield Co. shall be granted a seven (7) year distribution period, commencing_____.

2. Brand X Co. shall loan to the Art Greenfield Co. a ____ print/tape of each feature.

3. Art Greenfield Co. Shall receive a sales fee of thirty five percent (35%) of all gross contracts obtained and shall render quarterly statements to Brand X Co., covering all amounts received during the previous quarter and shall include an appropriate check for Brand X Co.'s sixty five percent (65%), first quarter ending____and quarterly thereafter.

4. Brand X Co. represents, warrants and agrees that they have the right to grant the rights herein being granted to Art Greenfield Co. with respect to the films/tapes and Brand X Co. further agrees to indemnify Art Greenfield Co. and hold Art Greenfield Co. harmless from and against any liability, loss, cost, damage or expense including attorney's fees, which arise from or in connection with or are in any way related to the distribution by Art Greenfield Co. of the films/tapes.

5. Brand X Co. understands that Art Greenfield Co. is distributing and agrees that Art Greenfield Co. may continue to distribute television programming for others, and specifically understands and agrees that at Art Greenfield Co.'s sole option and election, Art Greenfield Co. is currently distributing for television exhibition; providing only, that Art Greenfield Co. shall separately negotiate and bargain for the license fee for the films/tapes with the television station or stations involved as well as ancillary contracts.

6. Brand X Co. agrees that Art Greenfield Co. shall have the right to distribute the films in such manner and by such method or means as Art Greenfield Co. in their sole discretion shall determine, including the right to distribute the films/tapes through sub-licensees and that all decisions, with respect to such distribtu:on shall be made by the Art Greenfield Co. Brand X Co. further acknowledges and agrees that Art Greenfield Co. has made and makes no representation whatever with respect to the amount of distribution revenues or proceeds to be obtained by Art Greenfield Co. and that the royalty payable to Art Greenfield Co. hereunder shall be computed only upon gross proceeds, if any, retained or payable to Art Greenfield Co.'s sub-licensees.

7. Brand X Co. and Art Greenfield Co. mutually agree that even though a seven (7) year basic sales license has been granted to the Art Greenfield Co. herein Art Greenfield Co. or Brand X Co. may upon thirty (30) days written notice terminate this understanding. In the event either of these options is exercised all signed contracts obtained by Art Greenfield Co. to that point shall be honored with respect to the basic distribution fee understanding.

If the foregoing meets with your approval, please indicate your acceptance and agreement thereto by signing at the space provided below.

AGREED AND ACCEPTED TO:
ART GREENFIELD COMPANY

_____
Art Greenfield

BRAND X COMPANY

_____
X

Fig. 12-4. A sample distribution agreement covering television and ancillary television areas.

This agreement made this .... day of .... 19......, by and between ....

............, (hereinafter referred to as the Lessor) and

............, Licensee of Television Broadcast Station ....,

located in the city of ...., State of............
(hereinafter referred to as the Licensee)

1. GRANT: Lessor hereby grants, and Licensee accepts, a limited license, under the copyright of the pictures to telecast the films as specified in the following schedule to non-paying audiences only, over the television facilities of the above-named station:

SCHEDULE

TITLE OR SERIES	NO. OF FILMS	TOTAL NO. OF TELECASTS	STARTING DATE	ENDING DATE	PRICE PER (FILM-TELECAST)	LICENSE FEE FOR ENTIRE SERIES

Lessor grants the license to telecast over the broadcast facilities only of the station designated.

2. **PAYMENT**: Payment of $ .... on ....

   (date)

   Payment of $ .... on ....

   (date)

   until the entire license fee is paid.

3. **DELIVERY AND SHIPMENT**: Lessor shall make delivery of a 16mm positive synchronized print, or such optical film or magnetic tape as may currently be in use in the television industry, of each film of the series specified in the schedule. Such delivery will be made by common carrier or by mail in time for the prints to reach Licensee reasonably well in advance of the time of each scheduled telecast. All costs of such delivery shall be borne by Licensee. Licensee will reship each print in accordance with Lessor's directions at Licensee's expense within 48 hours after its telecast. Licensee agrees that all prints will be shipped in the same condition as when received, reasonable wear and tear due to proper use excepted. If the Licensee or its duly appointed agent, fails to return or delays the return of any print to the Lessor, or fails to forward, or delays forwarding (as directed by the Lessor) any such print to any other Licensee, the Licensee agrees to indemnify the Lessor or such other Licensee for any damage caused by said failure or delay.

4. **INSPECTION**: Licensee will examine each print upon delivery. If any print is not physically suitable for television transmission, Licensee will notify Lessor within 24 hours after the receipt of said print, so that Lessor may substitute a suitable print.

5. **DAMAGED PRINTS**: For each linear foot of any print lost, stolen or destroyed between the time of delivery thereof by Lessor and the return thereof by Licensee to the carrier, Licensee agrees to pay to Lessor the actual laboratory cost of replacement thereof, which payment, however, shall not transfer title in such print to Licensee or any other party.

6. **CUTS AND CREDITS**: Licensee may make minor cuts or eliminations from the prints, provided it restores each such cut or elimination without damage to said print. Licensee may not, however, eliminate any of the credits including stars, director, producer, distributor, writer and/or author, but must show these exactly as they appear on the positive print, nor may Licensee alter the title in any way, either on the print or in advertising the series, without prior written consent from the Lessor.

Fig. 12-5. Ancillary distributor contract.

7. **WARRANTIES:**

a. Lessor warrants that it has the right to grant the license for broadcasting the television films herein and that such broadcasting will not violate rights of others.

b. Lessor warrants that the performing rights in all musical compositions contained in all films are controlled by BMI, ASCAP or SESAC, or are in the public domain or are controlled by Lessor to the extent required for the purposes of this agreement.

c. Lessor agrees to indemnify and hold Licensee harmless from and against any claims, damages, liabilities, costs and expenses arising out of a breach of the above warranties, provided however, that Lessor reserves the right, at its option, of assuming the defense of any such claim or participating in the defense with Licensee. No settlement of such claim shall be made without Lessor's written approval secured in advance.

8. **PROMOTION:** Licensee shall have the right to use the names, biographies and likenesses of artists connected with the production of, or performance in, any film herein for advertising and promotion of the broadcast of said film, but not for the endorsement of any product or service of any sponsor or advertiser.

9. **BREACH OR DEFAULT:** If the Licensee violates any of the provisions of this agreement or becomes insolvent, or is adjudicated bankrupt, or executes an assignment for the benefit of creditors, or a Receiver is appointed for any of Licensee's property, or if Licensee violates any of the provisions of any other License agreement heretofore or hereafter made with Lessor, then in any of said events, Lessor may either (a) terminate this contract; or (b) terminate this and such other contracts; or (c) suspend delivery of further pictures hereunder (and if Lessor elects, also under any or all of such other contracts) pending compliance by Licensee. Said remedies shall be in addition to, and without prejudice of, any right or remedy Lessor has at law, in equity, or provided for elsewhere in this agreement, on account of any such violation or breach. If Licensee fails or refuses to pay any of the license fees called for under this or any such other contract, Lessor may declare such failure or refusal a breach of this entire contract, or a breach of this and such other contracts and Lessor shall have the right to forthwith stop shipment and delivery of any further films and to recover as damages therefor the amount payable as license fees of all pictures theretofore delivered and not paid for, and of all pictures delivery of which were stopped by Lessor by reason of such breach and not theretofore paid for Licensee will be responsible for any and all reasonable collection costs, including but not limited to attorney's fees as well as the maximum legal allowable interest on any unpaid balances under this and any other contract which Licensee may have with Lessor.

If Licensee shall telecast any of the pictures herein referred to prior to Licensee having duly executed and returned such executed contract copies to Lessor, then at Lessor's option, by giving notice in writing, this agreement shall be in full force and effect as if Licensee had duly executed this contract.

10. FORCE MAJEUBE: Neither party hereunder shall incur any liability hereunder because of the failure properly to deliver, or the inability to broadcast, any or all pictures hereunder due to actions or rules by any other governmental authority resulting in the diminution of television operations, acts of God, labor disputes, failure of broadcasting facilities or other similar causes beyond the control of the parties. In the event of the existence of the aforesaid events and conditions, Lessor may at its election extend the term of this agreement for such period of time that will enable Licensee to broadcast the affected picture. In the event such extensions exceed four (4) consecutive weeks for each thirteen (13) exhibitions licensed hereunder, Lessor shall have the right to terminate this agreement.

11. INTERPRETATION: This agreement shall be interpreted and enforced in all respects, in accordance with the laws of the State of California, and shall be deemed to have been executed in California. It represents the entire agreement between the parties and no modification or waiver of any term thereof shall be effective unless in writing and signed by both parties. The waiver by either party of any breach or default by the other party may not be construed as a waiver of any other breach or default by such other party.

12. TAXES: Licensee shall pay to Lessor the amount of all taxes and other fees imposed by any law now or hereafter in effect levied or based upon the license, delivery, exhibition, possession or use by Licensee of the prints of the films licensed hereunder or upon the grant of this license or the exercise thereof, or based upon or measured by the license fees or any part thereof. The failure by Lessor to collect any of the foregoing shall not be deemed a waiver of the right of Lessor to demand and collect the same at any time thereafter.

13. DUPLICATION: Licensee shall not copy or duplicate any prints or authorize or permit such duplication.

14. ASSIGNMENT: This agreement may not be assigned by the Licensee without the written consent of the Lessor secured in advance.

Fig. 12-5. Ancillary distributor contract (continued from page 170).

13. **ADDITIONAL TERMS:**

IN WITNESS WHEREOF, Licensee has on this day and year above written, executed this application, which, upon acceptance by Lessor by having it executed by one of its officers, shall constitute a license for the telecast of the pictures herein, in accordance with the terms and conditions hereof.

LICENSOR: LICENSEE:

BY.. BY..

Fig. 12-5. Ancillary distributor contract (continued from page 171).

The standard agreement covers the following:

■ The name, date and contract number of the agreement and the address of the television station.

■ The title of the picture, date of the telecast and the number of performances.

■ The running time and film width (16 mm, 35 mm or videotape) and the license fee. The term *substaining* means that the television station is paying for the motion picture with no income whatsoever. *Sponsored* means that the television station is receiving money for the telecast from a sponsor.

■ The contract has a place for the address of the television distributor and the television station. The contract is dated and signed by authorized personnel.

ANCILLARY TELEVISION

The dictionary defines *ancillary* as subordinate, subsidiary, supplementary. In the distribution industry, ancillary means that a film *comes across on a television screen.*

Tremendous strides have been made in the last few years in servicing this huge market. Ancillary is coming of age. It is a billion dollar industry and is growing daily. Most films today are being transferred to videotape and placed in video cassettes. Standard cassettes are in ¾″, ½″ or disc. They are sold for viewing in the following markets:

■ Hotels and motels
■ Hospitals
■ In-home use.
■ Pay for view television
■ Subscription television
■ Inflight-planes, boats, passenger liners, freighters, tuna boats, oil tankers and oil derricks.

Producers will find these markets very lucrative. They are able to turn their older films into profit-makers again.

PAY TELEVISION

Pay television means the transmission of images and sound through the air, by cable, by wire or by any other methods, systems or processes, whether or not now known or contemplated, to television receivers where reception is available only upon payment of a *per program* charge. Figure 12-3 is a pay television agreement between a pay TV station and a producer. A gross

Table 12-1. Playdate Results for a 10 Day Period.

The film was played on pay television per the agreement in Fig. 12-3. The royalty to the producer was 20 percent of the price charged.

DATE	EXHIBITIONS	NUMBER OF SUBSCRIBERS	PRICE CHARGED	$TOTAL
1-1-78	9:00 a.m.	53	$3.50	185.50
1-1-78	1:00 p.m.	124	3.50	434.00
1-1-78	6:00 p.m.	90	3.50	315.00
1-1-78	11:00 p.m.	266	3.50	931.00
1-2-78	11:00 a.m.	37	3.50	129.50
1-2-78	3:00 p.m.	74	3.50	259.00
1-2-78	8:00 p.m.	99	3.50	346.50
1-3-78	1:00 a.m.	101	3.50	353.50
1-3-78	9:00 a.m.	40	3.50	140.00
1-3-78	1:00 p.m.	73	3.50	255.50
1-3-78	6:00 p.m.	61	3.50	213.50
1-3-78	11:00 p.m.	3	3.50	10.50
1-4-78	11:00 a.m.	24	3.50	84.00
1-4-78	3:00 p.m.	45	3.50	157.50
1-4-78	8:00 p.m.	17	3.50	59.50
1-5-78	1:00 a.m.	78	3.50	273.00
1-5-78	9:00 a.m.	22	3.50	77.00
1-5-78	12:00 p.m.	44	3.50	154.00
1-5-78	6:00 p.m.	48	3.50	168.00
1-5-78	11:00 p.m.	109	3.50	381.50
1-6-78	3:00 p.m.	62	3.50	217.00
1-7-78	11:00 a.m.	30	3.50	105.00
1-7-78	6:00 p.m.	62	3.50	217.00
1-7-78	8:00 p.m.	123	3.50	430.50
1-8-78	1:00 a.m.	176	3.50	616.00
1-8-78	1:00 p.m.	53	3.50	185.50
1-9-78	9:00 a.m.	36	3.50	126.00
1-9-78	3:00 p.m.	64	3.50	224.00
1-9-78	11:00 p.m.	113	3.50	395.50
1-10-78	11:00 a.m.	44	3.50	154.00

receipts computation and payment form is found in Fig. 12-4. Table 12-1 breaks down the playdate results for a 10 day period.

Since ancillary television is potentially as great as a market as theatre exhibition, it is wise for the producer to contract with a professional distributor for distribution to these ancillary television outlets. This type of distributor is an expert in the field and is aware of the markets, terms and projections of income possible from these playdates.

Each market is different. It is almost impossible for a single producer to be in a position to contract all the inflights, hotels and motels, hospitals, in-home use, etc.

A distribution agreement (Fig. 12-5) covering television and ancillary television areas is an important agreement to study since the producer will have to familarize himself with the terms and conditions of the agreement. Following this distribution agreement the ancillary distributor then forms a contract (Fig. 12-6) for all markets. This contract is changed for each particular playdate but the terms and conditions remain basically the same.

Chapter 13

Additional Sales Markets

In addition to theatres and television, there are several other available markets which the distributor can contact for the possible exhibition of the motion picture.

ARMED SERVICE SALES

Probably the most obscure market available is the Armed Services. There is a great deal of paperwork involved as well as necessary approvals from Approval Officers.

Most distributors prefer to use an agent who specializes in this market. They work on a commission basis and are in daily contact with "the powers to be" at the reviewing offices.

Each service has a different procedure and a different approval. The U.S. Navy deals in 16 mm color prints. If the Navy approves the film, they want 40 prints of the motion picture. Unless one works through an agent, it will be necessary to lay out laboratory costs for the 40 prints. Once the Navy inspects the prints and approves same, then payment will be made. Through the agent, all details as far as laboratory costs, etc. are taken care of and the distributor receives the net profit from the sale. The net profit—after payment of commission and all expenses—will come between a minimum of $6,000.00 and a maximum of $10,200.00 for this sale. This is not too much income but it is like "found money" since it does not compete with domestic sales.

The U.S. Army and the Air Force deal in 35 mm color films. These are normal release prints from the laboratory. These prints are shown in the PX's around the country. The Army and Air Force require 40 prints in 26 exchange areas in the United States. They will use the prints for five weeks. The net profit— after payment of commission and all expenses—will come between a minimum of $3,000.00 and a maximum of $20,000.00 depending on the drawing power of the motion picture.

The Army and Air Force also show motion pictures abroad in the PX's. Overseas viewing is a combination of 16 mm color film and 35 mm color film. Net profit—after payment of commission and all expenses—will come between a minimum of $250.00 and a maximum of $4,000.00.

Armed Service Sales should only be made when the motion picture prints are dormant or have had extensive runs in the United States and abroad and the prints are not in use. This gives the distributor extra income and does not interfere with normal booking procedures. Also, the prints can be in number three condition.

A recapitulation of income from Armed Service Sales comes between a minimum of $9250.00 and a maximum of $34,200.00.

The American Forces Radio and Television service serves 1-1/2 million U.S. Military and DoD Civilian employees and their families overseas through stations operated by Army, Navy and Air Force Commands. There is a good market in this field. They purchase discs, tapes and film programs. They require basically ¾ inch video tape cassettes instead of film.

It is interesting to note that the AFRTS pays the same amount of money for all films regardless of production costs or production companies. An independent with an acceptable film costing $100,000 would receive the same income from this organization as Universal-International would receive for their block-buster "JAWS." This makes the market very available and lucrative for the independent film producer.

All Armed Services demand that each motion picture must first be screened. These services have screening facilities available for both 16 mm and 35 mm films as well as cassettes. The film producer pays all screening print transportation costs.

Since this can be a ready market for the producer it is well to spend time and effort reviewing each of the Armed Forces.

DEPARTMENTS OF THE ARMY AND THE AIR FORCE

This organization is headquartered at Dallas, Texas and is the procurement agency for both the Army and the Air Force.

Basically, they show films at PXs both here in the states and at Army and Air Force Bases throughout the world. The AAFES utilizes 35 mm commercial prints for domestic circuits with payment based on a negotiated percentage of grosses. The various AAFES shipping depots are listed in Table 13-1.

It is the responsibility of the Producer to have a shipping depot in each of the cities listed on Table 13-1 so that AAFES carriers can pick up the prints and deliver them to the theatres. In turn, the carriers return the prints to the shipping depots after use.

Should the film be selected for AAFES overseas circuits as well, the requirements are for ten 35 mm prints (new or rejuvenated) and 22 new 16 mm prints. For late show and matinee overseas circuit use, six and five rejuvenated 35 mm prints respectively are required. No 16 mm prints are used on these circuits. The producer must have legal non-theatrical distribution rights for the United States as well as for overseas U.S. Military use. Further, all prints must have a MPAA rating logo.

The general provisions applicable to orders for rental of motion pictures and related items by the Army and Air Force Exchange Service are found in Fig.13-1. The determination of film rental terms for the use of domestic prints and the procurement of overseas prints is outlined in the *Availability Agreement* (Fig. 13-2) of the Department of the Army and the Air Force.

DEPARTMENT OF THE NAVY

The least amount of effort and paper work is involved when dealing with the Department of the Navy. However, like all of the Armed Forces, the Navy does require that the producer adhere to certain regulations.

The producer must have legal theatrical distribution rights for the United States as well as for overseas U.S. Military use. He must also submit the film for approval and viewing.

The award of the contract (Fig. 13-3) is made by the Bureau of Naval Personnel, Department of the Navy, Washington, D.C. 20370. The producer should submit the film for viewing and approval to the Navy Motion Picture Service, Building 311, Flushing Avenue, Brooklyn, New York 11251.

If the film is approved, the Navy will purchase outright between 40 and 45 16 mm prints of the film. The film will be leased for a rental period of 36 months from the date of delivery of such prints. After the 36 month period, the Navy will then deliver to the producer the used prints at its office or designated exchange in New York City.

Until quite recently, the Navy used these 16 mm prints in their exchanges in the United States and their ships at sea. However, for overseas viewing, the American Forces Radio and Television Service has been servicing the ships at sea. Currently, there are over 160 Navy ships with closed circuit television and these ships have converted to cassette videotapes. In the very near future, these ships will be receiving these films through their own satellite. This may affect the number of prints the Navy will require but there are still over 900 Naval establishments in the United States viewing the 16 mm films.

AMERICAN ARMED FORCES RADIO AND TELEVISION SERVICE

The objective of American Forces Radio and Television Service is to furnish the Armed Forces with the best available programs for broadcast both for information and entertainment.

The AFRTS broadcasts television programs as well as feature motion pictures. They cover sports, religious programs, variety, drama, feature films, fillers, cartoons and short subjects. They do not discriminate on the source of material nor where this material comes from. It offers an equal opportunity to all producers, big or small. They also pay the same price for broadcast rights.

The AFTRS is only for non-commercial broadcasts outside the United States and does not conflict with theatrical or commercial television. Also AFTRS agrees to limit the distribution of videotapes to a single run through its television circuits and to erase them upon their return to AFTRS-LA. AFTRS will maintain strict control over the accounting for all copies made in-house or by a commercial duplicating contractor.

The price is set by the AFTRS and an interested producer can contact this organization at the following address:

American Forces Radio and Television Service
1016 N. McCadden Place
Los Angeles, CA 90038

Upon receipt of your material they will evaluate it and if they approve your motion picture product, they will issue an award similar to the one in Fig. 13-4.

FOREIGN SALES

Usually foreign sales are sold outright for U.S. dollars at a negotiated flat price. The selling price is based on the population of the purchasing country and the ability of the foreign buyer to make

Table 13-1. AAFES Shipping Depots.

EXCHANGE REGION / MOTION PICTURE OFFICE	NUMBER OF PRINTS REQUIRED	MAXIMUM NO. DAYS PRINT REQUIRED 1	2	3	4	5	6
Alamo Exchange Region (ALER) San Antonio, Tx	6	53	53	52	45	51	44
Dallas , Tx							
Capitol Exchange Region (CPER) Alexandria, VA							
Albany, NY	1	36	x	x	x	x	x
Boston, MA	1	42	13	x	x	x	x
New York, NY	1	44	x	x	x	x	x
(1) Philadelphia, PA	2	72	75	x	x	,x	x
Washington, D.C.	3	49	49	44	x	x	x
Golden Gate Exchange Region (GGER) San Francisco, CA							
Los Angeles, CA	2	55	51	x	x	x	x
Salt Lake City, UT	1	44	x	x	x	x	x
(2) Settle, WA	2	43	130		x	x	x
San Francisco, CA	2	56	48	x	x	x	x
Ohio Valley Exchange Region (OVER) Charlestown, IN							
Cincinnati, OH	1	64	x	x	x	x	x
Indianapolis, IN	2	71	69	x	x	x	x
Kansas City, MO	2	62	62	x	x	x	x
Omaha, NE	1	49	x	x	x	x	x
Denver, CO	2	42	42	x	x	x	x
Southeast Exchange Region (SEER) Montgomery, AL							
(3) Atlanta, GA	6	49	49	56	56	63	70
TOTAL	35						

(1) Philadelphia-print 1 includes Lajes AB, Azores. Print 2 includes the Northeast-Thule and Sondrestrom AFB

(2) Seattle-print 2 is the Alaska circuit.

(3) Print 6 includes St. Buchanan, Puerto Rico

Change # - 28 Mar 78 Boston requires only one print changing total to 35 prints

Table 13-1. AAFES Shipping Depots (continued from page 180).

As you will notice they require 35 prints, and these print requirements are as follows:

EFFECTIVE
5 Mar 78

35 MM PRINT REQUIREMENT - DOMESTIC SPECIAL CIRCUITS

NUMBER OF PRINTS REQUIRED

	SPECIAL MATINEE	LATE SHOW
ALAMO EXCHANGE REGION (ALER)	6	6
Dallas		
CAPITOL EXCHANGE REGION (CPER)		
Albany	1	0
Boston	1	1
New York	1	1
Philadelphia	2	1
Washington, D.C.	3	1
GOLDEN GATE EXCHANGE REGION (GGER)		
Los Angeles	2	1
Salt Lake City	1	1
Seattle	*2	1
San Francisco	2	1
OHIO VALLEY EXCHANGE REGION (OVER)		
Cincinnati	1	1
Indianapolis	2	2
Kansas City	2	2
Denver	2	1
Omaha	1	1
SOUTHEAST EXCHANGE REGION (SEER)		
Atlanta	6	4
TOTALS	35	25

*One print is for Alaska circuit

ARMY AND AIR FORCE EXCHANGE SERVICE

DALLAS, TEXAS 75222

GENERAL PROVISIONS

APPLICABLE TO ORDERS FOR
RENTAL OF MOTION PICTURES AND RELATED ITEMS
BY THE ARMY AND AIR FORCE EXCHANGE SERVICE
(AAFES)

This booklet contains the General Provisions which apply to orders for rental of motion pictures and related items by AAFES. This booklet will not be included in each Film Rental Order or Print and Advertising Order but will be incorporated by reference. All provisions contained herein will be applicable to each order issued. If you have any questions about these provisions, please contact the Contracting Officer shown on the order. He will be happy to assist you in any way possible.

ARMY AND AIR FORCE EXCHANGE SERVICE
GENERAL PROVISIONS
(Rental of Motion Pictures and Related Services)

1. **DEFINITIONS:** As used throughout this contract the following terms shall have the meaning set forth below:

   a. "AAFES" identifies the Army and Air Force Exchange Service.

   b. The term "Contract" means all types of agreements and orders including purchase orders for the procurement of merchandise, supplies, services and/or equipment. It includes amendments and supplemental agreements with respect to any of the foregoing.

   c. "Contracting Officer" means the person executing or administering this contract on behalf of AAFES or his successor or successors.

   d. The term "Contractor" means an individual, partnership, corporation or other entity responsible for the execution of a contract to provide goods and/or services at a certain price or rate. This includes the term "Vendor", "Seller", or "Distributor."

2. **LEGAL STATUS:** The Army and Air Force Exchange Service, including its activities, offices, individual exchanges and overseas exchange systems, is an integral part of the Departments of the Army and the Air Force and is an instrumentality of the United States Government. Army and Air Force Exchange Service contracts are United States contracts; however, they do not obligate appropriated funds of the United States except for a judgment or compromise settlement in suits brought in the Federal District courts (28 USC 1346) and in the United States Court of Claims (28 USC 1491), in which event the Army and Air Force Exchange Service will reimburse the United States Government, (31 USC 724(a).) (NOTE: The Armed Services Procurement Act applies only to procurements for which payment is to be made from appropriated funds (10 USC 2303(a)) and does not govern AAFES procurements. The Armed Services Procurement Regulations (ASPR), promulgated pursuant to the Armed Services Procurement Act, are likewise inapplicable except for those ASPR provisions that have been procedurally adopted by AAFES and that are either incorporated into or specifically referenced in this contract.)

Fig. 13-1. AAFES general provisions.

3. DISPUTES: Except as otherwise provided in this contract, any dispute concerning a question of fact arising under this contract which is not disposed of by agreement shall be decided by the Contracting Officer, who shall reduce his decision to writing and mail or otherwise furnish a copy thereof to the Contractor. The decision of the Contracting Officer shall be final and conclusive unless, within 30 days from the date of receipt of such copy, the Contractor mails or otherwise furnishes to the Contracting Officer a written appeal addressed to the Armed Services Board of Contract Appeals. The decision of the Board shall be final and conclusive unless determined by a United States court of competent jurisdiction to have been fraudulent, or capricious, or arbitrary or so grossly erroneous as necessarily to imply bad faith, or not supported by substantial evidence. In connection with any appeal proceeding under this clause, the Contractor shall be afforded an opportunity to be heard and to offer evidence in support of his appeal. Pending final decision of a dispute hereunder, the Contractor shall proceed diligently with the performance of the contract and in accordance with the Contracting Officer's decision. This 'Disputes' clause does not preclude the consideration of law questions in connection with decisions provided for herein; provided, that nothing in this contract shall be construed as making final the decision of any administrative official, representative or Board on a question of law.

4. GRATUITIES AND CONTINGENT FEES: Contractor warrants that no person or selling agency has been employed or retained to secure this contract upon an agreement or understanding for a commission, percentage, brokerage, or contingent fee excepting bona fide employees or bona fide established commercial selling agencies retained by Contractor for the purpose of securing business. Contractor warrants that no gratuities (entertainment, gifts, etc.) were or will be offered or given by the Contractor or any person representing the Contractor to any AAFES officer or employee or any other officer or employee of the United States Government to secure this contract or favorable treatment with respect to this contract. For breach of either of the warranties, AAFES may terminate the contract for default and deduct from amounts due under this or other contracts, or bill Contractor for, the total value of any contingent fee or gratuity.

5. REPRESENTATIONS: The Contractor will not represent himself to be an agent or representative of the AAFES, the United States, or any military department.

6. HOLD AND SAVE HARMLESS: Contractor shall at all times hold and save harmless the United States and the AAFES, its agents, representatives and employees from any and all suits, claims, charges and expenses which arise out of acts or omissions of Contractor, its agents, representatives or employees.

7. PURCHASES FROM RHODESIA AND CERTAIN COMMUNIST AREAS: Contractor shall not acquire for use in the performance of this contract or any subcontract thereunder any supplies originating from sources within Rhodesia, or any supplies which originated in, or were transferred from or through North Korea, North Vietnam, or Cuba (except supplies which have been lawfully imported into the United States, its possessions, or Puerto Rico).

8. **MODIFICATIONS AND ADDITIONS:** Except for unilateral written amendments signed by the Contracting Officer which may be authorized in this contract, all changes, modifications, additions, or deletions to this contract must be prepared in writing as formal amendments signed by both parties and approved in accordance with provisions of applicable regulations.

9. <u>TERMINATION</u>: Relative to termination of this contract, it is mutually agreed:

a. This contract may be terminated in whole or in part by either party immediately upon written notice to the other party in the event of breach or violation of the conditions of this contract by said other party.

b. This contract may be terminated in whole or in part by either party upon thirty (30) days' notice in writing to the other party.

10. <u>PERMITS AND LICENSES:</u> Contractor will at his own expense, obtain all necessary permits, give all notices, pay all license fees, and comply with all laws, rules, ordinances, and regulations relating to the preservation of the public health or applicable to the service or business carried on under this contract. The burden of determining applicability of licensing requirements, laws, ordinances, and regulations for contractor and his employees rests with the contractor.

11. <u>TAXES:</u> The prices herein reflect full reduction for taxes which are nonapplicable. In addition to exemption from Federal excise taxes by virtue of exportation, all tangible personal property sold to Army Post Exchanges, Air Force Base Exchanges, and Army and Air Force Exchange Service for resale is exempt from state sales and use taxes. All sales other than for resale depend on state law or federal constitutional immunity for exemption from state sales or use taxes.

12. <u>ASSIGNMENT/TRANSFER:</u> Contractor may not assign the conduct of his business or operation under this contract, or transfer his rights or delegate his obligations thereunder without first obtaining a prior written consent of the Contracting Officer. No assignment or transfer, no matter how accomplished, shall be effective, nor shall any assignee or transferee acquire any rights to or under this contract unless a consent to any such assignment or transfer is obtained from the Contracting Officer. The Contracting Officer will make a determination as to whether or not consent will be made as to the assignment or transfer of the contract and will so advise the contractor. If Contracting Officer's consent is given to such assignment or transfer, the contract will be modified accordingly. Furthermore, contractor shall promptly advise the Contracting Officer of any impending merger, consolidation, reorganization or change in name involving the contractor, and will furnish the Contracting Officer such proof as may be required by the Contracting Officer sufficient to show that all terms and conditions of the contract will continue to be fully performed. Failure of contractor to comply with the requirements of this paragraph will form a basis for immediate termination of the contract pursuant to paragraph 9 of these General Provisions.

Fig. 13-1. AAFES general provisions (continued from page 184).

13. **CLAIMS BY CONTRACTOR:** No claim by Contractor arising out of the performance or termination of this contract will be considered by AAFES unless such claim will have been submitted in writing to the Contracting Officer not later than (90) days following effective date of termination or expiration of this contract.

14. **NONWAIVER OF DEFAULTS:** Any failure by AAFES at any time or from time to time to enforce or require strict performance of any terms or conditions of this contract will not constitute waiver thereof and will not affect or impair such terms and conditions in any way or AAFES's right at any time to avail itself of such remedies as it may have for any such breach or breaches of such terms and conditions.

15. **EXAMINATION OF RECORDS:** a. This clause is applicable if the amount of this contract exceeds $2,500 and was entered into by means of negotiation. The Contractor agrees that the Contracting Officer or his duly authorized representatives shall have the right to examine and audit the books and records of the Contractor directly pertaining to the contract during the period of the contract and until and expiration of three years after final payment under the contract.

  b. The Contractor agrees to include the clause in (a) in all his subcontracts hereunder, except purchase orders not exceeding $2,500.

16. **ADVERTISEMENTS:** The Contractor will not represent in any manner, expressly or by implication, that products purchased under this contract are approved or endorsed by any element of the United States Government. Any advertisement, including cents-off coupons, by the Contractor which refers to a military resale activity will contain a statement that the advertisement was neither paid for nor sponsored, in whole or in part, by the particular activity.

17. **EQUAL EMPLOYMENT OPPORTUNITY.**

  a. The contractor agrees to comply with regulations of the Department of Labor contained in Title 41, Code of Federal Regulations, Chapter 60, which are incorporated herein by reference.

  b. A contract award in the amount of $1,000,000 or more will not be made unless the Contractor, and each first-tier subcontractor which will receive a subcontract of $1,000,000 or more, are found on the basis of a review to be in compliance with the Equal Employment Opportunity regulations of the Department of Labor.

18. **AFFIRMATIVE ACTION FOR DISABLED VETERANS AND VETERANS OF THE VIETNAM ERA.** If this contract equals or exceeds $10,000.00, and is not otherwise exempt, the contractor agrees to comply with the regulations of the Department of Labor and the Office of Federal Contract Compliance Program, and the Affirmative Action clause as set out in Title 41, Code of Federal Regulations, Part 60-250, which are incorporated herein by reference.

19. AFFIRMATIVE ACTION FOR HANDICAPPED WORKERS. If this contract equals or exceeds $2,500, and is not otherwise exempt, the contractor agrees to comply with the regulations of the Department of Labor and the Affirmative Action clause as set out in Title 41, Code of Federal Regulations, Part 60-741, which are incorporated herein by reference.

20. CONVICT LABOR: In connection with the performance of work under this contract the Contractor agrees not to employ any person undergoing sentence of imprisonment except as provided by Public Law 89-176, September 10, 1965 (18 USC 4082(c)(2)) and Executive Order 11755, December 29, 1973.

21. ENVIRONMENTAL PROTECTION.

a. This clause shall apply to any contract in excess of $100,000, indefinite quantity contracts estimated to exceed $100,000 in one year; provided, however, it shall not apply to use of facilities located outside the United States or to contracts otherwise excepted in accordance with 40 CFR part 15.

b. Unless this contract is exempt, by acceptance of this contract, Contractor (and where appropriate subcontractor) stipulates:

(1) that any facility to be utilized in the performance of any nonexempt contract or subcontract is not listed on the EPA List of Violating Facilities as of the date of contract award.

(2) his (their) agreement to comply with all requirements of section 114 of the Air Act and section 308 of the Water Act relating to inspection, monitoring, entry, reports, and information, as well as all other requirements specified in section 114 and 308 of the Air Act and the Water Act, respectively, and all regulations and guidelines issued thereunder.

(3) that as a condition of award of contract, he shall promptly notify the Contracting Officer of the receipt of any communication from the Director, Office of Federal Activities, U.S. Environmental Protection Agency, or his delegee, indicating that a facility to be utilized for the contract is under consideration to be listed on the EPA List of Violating Facilities.

(4) his (their) agreement to include the criteria and requirements in subparagraphs (1) through (4) in every nonexempt subcontract, and to take such action as the Government may direct as a means of enforcing such provisions.

Fig. 13-1. AAFES general provisions (continued from page 186).

ARMY AND AIR FORCE EXCHANGE SERVICE
AVAILABILITY AGREEMENT
(RENTAL OF MOTION PICTURES AND/OR RELATED ITEMS)

AVAILABILITY AGREEMENT NO.

ISSUED BY	DATE

1. This agreement consisting of Availability Agreement, AAFES FORM 6900-78, and the attached Schedule, AAFES FORM 4450-9, pages _____ through _____ establishes terms and conditions for future rental of motion pictures and/or related items as required by AAFES.

2. The terms and conditions of this agreement will apply to each Film Rental Order or Print and Advertising Order placed with the distributor. As requirements are determined, AAFES will negotiate specific items, quantities, destination/delivery points, delivery dates, and any special provisions not contained or referenced in this agreement. In addition to the provisions contained herein, the General Provisions referenced in the order will apply.

3. When the agreement is signed by both parties, it shall constitute an agreement between the distributor indicated hereon and the AAFES whereby distributor agrees to furnish items and perform services required by this agreement, any amendments hereto and any order issued hereafter.

DISTRIBUTOR		
FULL NAME AND ADDRESS OF DISTRIBUTOR	SIGNATURE	DATE
	TYPED NAME AND TITLE	
	TELEPHONE NUMBER	

CONTRACTING OFFICER		
TYPED NAME	SIGNATURE	DATE

APPROVAL		
TYPED NAME AND TITLE	SIGNATURE	DATE

AAFES FORM 6900–78 (REV DEC 77) (PREV EDITION OBSOLETE)

Fig. 13-2. AAFES availability agreement.

FILM AVAILABILITY AGREEMENT (16MM and 35MM)

1. **AVAILABILITY OF FILM:**

The Distributor will furnish from its available film product the features and short subjects selected by AAFES. A film is considered available upon manufacture of the first positive 35MM print for commercial release, except that the Distributor shall not be required to deliver prints of available film product to AAFES in advance of the published release date in the United States. The Distributor will, wherever possible, have 35MM positive prints manufactured for AAFES use at the same time as those prints which are required for distribution in the continental United States, that is, domestic prints. Prints will be promptly delivered to AAFES after selection and availability. It is understood that delivery by the Distributor of prints will be subject to delivery capability of the printing laboratories.

2. **NUMBER OF PRINTS:**

a. Twenty-two 16MM prints of each subject will be provided for exhibition by AAFES in oversea and remote domestic locations. Oversea locations are defined as locations outside the continental U.S. for which separate prints are ordered specifically for the use of AAFES. Domestic remote locations are defined as locations within the continental U.S. for which 16MM prints are ordered specifically for the use of AAFES.

b. Ten 35MM prints of each subject will be provided for exhibition by AAFES in oversea locations.

c. Forty-two 35MM prints of each subject will be made available to AAFES by the Distributor for exhibition in domestic locations (excluding remote locations) unless a different quantity for a specific film or a different releasing arrangement is agreed upon. Domestic locations are defined as locations on 35MM circuits for which films are made available to AAFES by the Distributor at commercial Film Exchanges within the continental United States.

3. PACKING OF PRINTS:

a. All feature and short subject prints as outlined in 2a and b will be packed unmounted and on cores with reel bands attached, unless otherwise requested by the Film Procurement Branch, AAFES. AAFES will pay for the actual cost of reels and shipping cases if the method of packing requested by the Film Procurement Branch, AAFES, requires such materials.

b. 35MM prints for domestic use excluding remote locations will be made available on shipping reels in ICC containers.

4. DELIVERY AND RETURN OF PRINTS:

a. 35MM domestic prints will be delivered by the Distributor, at his expense; to the shipping depot for pick-up by the AAFES transportation agent. Transportation to and between AAFES theaters, and return to the shipping depot from AAFES theaters will be arranged and paid by AAFES.

Fig. 13-2. AAFES availability agreement (continued from page 190).

b. Transportation of all prints, except in "a" above, to the AAFES receiving activity will normally be made via fourth class U.S. mail; however, it may be necessary at times to ship via other means. The film rental rates shall be deemed to include the prepaid costs of fourth class United States (U.S.) mail delivery to the first AAFES receiving activity. The Distributor will be reimbursed, upon request, the cost difference if a more expensive method of transportation is directed to be used by the film purchase/delivery order (AAFES Form 6900-51).

c. Prints used for oversea showings will be destroyed after use by the AAFES unless alternate instructions are furnished by the Distributor. Any return of prints or alternate disposition instructions will be accomplished at the expense of the Distributor.

5. **EXHIBITION AREAS:**

All subjects may be exhibited only under military auspices in areas under control of the U.S. Government, except that free exhibition will not be held at any place within three miles of a commercially operated motion picture theater, or a paid-admission theater operated by the Departments of the Army or the Air Force unless waiver is granted by special agreement between the Distributor or its affiliate company and the local commercial exhibitor (including AAFES) of 35MM or 16MM motion pictures.

6. PATRONAGE ELIGIBILITY:

Patronage eligibility for admission to AAFES theaters will be as outlined in AR 28-62/AFR 34-32 which will be superseded by AR 60-10/AFR 147-7.

7. PERIOD OF EXHIBITION:

The period of exhibition will be as follows except that, if prints finish their circuits and use prior to the expiration of the period of exhibition, they will be disposed of in accordance with the provisions of this agreement unless they are retained for repeat showings as defined herein:

a. 35MM films for domestic use will be availabl~ for the time required to complete the AAFES domestic circuit.

b. All films provided specifically for the AAFES use will not be exhibited in excess of 24 months following the date of delivery of the last print of a title unless an extension is agreed to by the Distributor.

8. PRINT REPLACEMENT:

Upon certification by AAFES that any print delivered hereunder has been lost or destroyed, the Distributor, if requested, will when possible replace such print, at the expense of the AAFES, provided the negative of such lost or destroyed print is available. The Distributor will effect prompt adjustment or replacement, at no cost to AAFES, of incomplete prints, duplicate reels or footage or any portion of a print damaged in transit from the Distributor to the receiving AAFES activity.

Fig. 13-2. AAFES availability agreement (continued from page 192).

9. **PAYMENT:**

AAFES will make all payments including feature minimum guarantees and flat rentals due the Distributor under the terms of this agreement in United States dollars in the United States within sixty (60) days after receipt of invoice and prints. Domestic and oversea film rental earnings reports will be made periodically (at least four times a month), at which time earnings including amount in excess of oversea minimum guarantees will be remitted to the Distributor.

10. **REPEAT FEATURE PRICE CLASSIFICATIONS:**

The effective price classification as set forth in subparagraph 10e will be used as the basis for determining the rates applicable to repeat showings. Pictures originally classified at 45% and 50% may be exhibited on a repeat basis during the period of exhibition as set forth in paragraph 7 of this agreement at 30% terms, and pictures originally classified at 40% and under may be exhibited on a repeat basis during the period of exhibition set forth in paragraph 7 at 25% terms. Pictures exhibited subsequent to completion of the first circuit of AAFES theaters will be considered repeat showing. Exceptions to the provisions of this paragraph may be made the subject of separate negotiations by either party.

11. RENTAL SCHEDULE FOR SHORT SUBJECTS:

a. Short subjects for 16MM domestic and 16MM and 35MM oversea will be paid on a flat rental per title in accordance with the following schedule, which includes twenty-two 16MM prints and ten 35MM prints: 1-reel short, $500.00; 2-reel short, $1,000.00.

b. In addition to the flat rental for short subjects as outlined above, the AAFES will pay for the cost of manufacturing the required number of prints or at the AAFES option will negotiate separately with film laboratories for the manufacture of the prints with the negative being supplied by the Distributor.

c. In the event the number of 16MM and 35MM prints of a feature subject is increased or decreased, the flat rental will be increased or reduced by $12.00 per reel for each 16MM print and $25.00 per reel for each 35MM print.

d. 35MM short subjects for domestic use will be the subject of separate negotiations using prints from the Distributor's available stocks.

12. SPECIAL RENTAL:

A flat payment of $50.00 per feature program will be made for KATUSA (Korean Augmentation to U.S. Army) free-admissions as authorized herein.

Fig. 13-2. AAFES availability agreement (continued from page 194).

13. ADVERTISING:

a. Advertising (trailers, one-sheets, stills and advertising mats) for the oversea areas will be provided to the AAFES by the Distributor at its cost for each feature subject provided under the terms of this agreement.

b. Advertising (trailers, one-sheets, stills and advertising mats) for domestic use will be ordered separately by AAFES from the distributor or its authorized source.

c. Advertising normally furnished to commercial motion picture exhibitors without charge will also be provided to the AAFES without charge.

14. DUPLICATION OF PRINTS:

AAFES will not duplicate any prints delivered hereunder or otherwise permit others to duplicate or exhibit such prints, except as provided in paragraphs 10 and 12.

15. TITLE TO FILM:

Title to the film subjects provided for hereunder and the prints, negatives, and copyrights thereof, shall at all times remain with the Distributor or its affiliated companies.

16. LICENSE:

The Distributor grants, and warrants that it has full authority to grant, for the purposes and uses described in this Availability Agreement, and for the consideration herein described as "film rental", a non exclusive worldwide license to AAFES in and to the film or any other copyrighted items which are ordered and delivered, pursuant to the Print and Advertising Order/Delivery Order, AAFES Form 6900-51 or Film Rental Purchase Order, AAFES Form 6900-77, and incorporating the terms of this Availability Agreement by reference.

17. ALTERATIONS:

Paragraph 10 on pages 3 and 4 is deleted. The following paragraph is substituted in its place:

FEATURE PRICE CLASSIFICATIONS:

a. Oversea 16MM and 35MM:

(1) Price classifications for films will be established by negotiation between the AAFES contracting officer and the distributor and confirmed by a Film Rental Purchase Order. Film rental for paid-admission showings will be computed on the basis of total gross receipts times the applicable effective price classification, subject to the provisions of (2) through (6) below.

(2) Film rental for prints manufactured for AAFES use in oversea areas shall be subject to the minimum guarantees established in subparagraph (4) below for the

Fig. 13-2. AAFES availability agreement (continued from page 196).

197

applicable price classification, and color print cost differential specified in (5) below when applicable. Minimum guarantees and color print cost differential paid by AAFES will be deducted from film rental earned prior to any film rental being paid by AAFES.

(3) Film rental for 16MM free-admission showings will be computed on the basis of free-admission attendance times the applicable rate per person as indicated in (4) below.

(4) The following schedule establishes effective price classifications, minimum guarantees and free admission rental rates for sixteen 16MM and ten 35MM black and white prints for oversea areas. If the oversea military population varies 10 percent upward or downward, negotiations will be conducted to make equitable adjustment to the minimum guarantee.

PRICE CLASSIFICATIONS	FEATURE MINIMUM GUARANTEE	16MM FREE ADMISSION RATES PER PERSON
20%	$ 4,550	$.03
25%	5,050	.0375
30%	5,800	.045
35%	7,300	.0525
40%	8,800	.06
45%	10,300	.0675
50%	11,500	.075

(5) For features printed in color, a print cost differential will be paid in addition to the minimum guarantee. The print cost differential is the difference in cost to the distributor between black and white and color film. For the purpose of computing the print cost differential, the rate established for black and white film is _____ per foot for 16MM and _____ for 35MM.

(6) In the event that the number of 16MM or 35MM prints of a feature subject is increased or decreased, the minimum guarantee in (4) above will be increased or decreased by $125 for each 16MM print and $225 for each 35MM print.

b. Domestic 16MM:

(1) Black and white 16MM feature subjects will be leased for a flat rate of $160 for each print ordered. Black and white footage costs in excess of two cents per foot may be added to the flat rate.

(2) Color 16MM feature subjects will be leased for a flat rate of $175 for features of less than 125 minutes running time; $200 for features of 125 minutes to 150 minutes; $225 for features in excess of 150 minutes. In addition, the print cost differential between black and white and color will be added to the flat rate. For the purpose of computing the print cost differential, the rate established for 16MM black and white film in a(5) above will be used.

c. Domestic 35MM: Price classifications for films will be established by negotiation between the AAFES contracting officer and the distributor and confirmed by a Film Rental Purchase Order. Film rental for all showings will be computed on the basis of total gross receipts times the applicable price classification. Film rental for prints furnished from distributors' domestic stock for AAFES use in the continental U.S. will be subject to a minimum charge of $7.50 per showday.

Fig. 13-2. AAFES availability agreement (continued from page 198).

a profit. Countries like England, Germany or Italy can pay more for a motion picture than countries like Egypt, India or Mexico.

Other factors also enter into the sale. These are often problems of currency restrictions where a country has a limited amount of hard currency and the motion picture import is low on the priority list of essentials. Another case is found in France where that country is high on national product and only allows a certain amount of foreign imports. Government censorship and approval also play a vital role in these sales. An example of this is Sweden—they will not allow any violence on the motion picture screen.

Payment for films is usually made through a foreign bank with a corresponding bank in the United States. Payment is made via *Irrevocable Letters of Credit in U.S. Dollars*. The letter of credit can be divisional and transferable but in order to collect the dollar amount, the seller must furnish the United States bank with certain items stipulated in the letter of credit. These include:

- One color 35 mm print in sync sound.
- One color 35 mm trailer in sync sound.
- All available advertising work including a certain number of pressbooks and one sheets.
- Foreign continuity script of the motion picture.

There are cancellation clauses which void the sale if the foreign buyer does not get Government approval or an import license. A typical foreign sales agreement between the buyer and the seller is found in Fig. 13-5.

Notice on this agreement that the first paragraph contains the date, the licensor's name (seller) and the licensee's name (buyer). Paragraph one lists the period of exhibition of the film in the country, the name of the motion picture and the territory of sale.

Paragraph two contains the purchase price of the motion picture and the terms of payment.

Paragraph 12 contains the *censor clause*. Under this paragraph the buyer (licensee) might want an added clause stating that if the picture is not approved by the censor in that country, then all costs will be refunded.

Finally, both the licensor and the licensee affix their signatures to the agreement.

Thus, a legal contract is in force. There is the date of the contract, the terms, financial considerations, and a time period.

Foreign Percentage Deal with Buyer

Occasionally, the seller may elect to make a distribution percentage agreement with the foreign buyer. This is true in countries like Canada, England and Australia. In that case, the buyer is considered an exchange of the seller. This agreement is the same as the one in Fig. 13-5 except that the distribution percentage arrangement is also listed.

Foreign Representative of the Distributor

The distributor has the option of selling directly to foreign countries or employing the services of a foreign sales representative. The foreign sales representative specializes in the foreign sales of the motion picture product.

Most distributors, especially if they are independent, prefer to use the services of a foreign representative. They understand the market and are aware of the requirements of each country. They also have contact with buyers.

An agreement between the distributor and the foreign sales agent (Fig. 13-6) is limited to a certain time period only. This foreign representation agreement covers the date of the agreement between the seller (distributor) and the foreign agent. The seller warrants that he is the exclusive owner (or has representation authority) to make the agreement and the seller lists the film in question. The agreement has a time limitation on representation and a financial consideration which is usually a percentage of each sale. Thus, we have another legal contract. We have the date of the contract, the terms, financial considerations and a time period.

Unless the distributor has an extensive list of buyers, it is sometimes wise to use a foreign representative. They usually work on a commission basis and the distributor has the option of approving all sales prior to commitment.

Many times, the sale commission is lower than what it would cost the distributor if he were to expend the time, money and traveling costs to make a foreign sale. Additionally, in many countries, there are various means of remunerations which are necessary for the approval of the sale in a foreign country. Usually the distributor would not be aware of this and he would not be able to make the sale.

Foreign sales can represent up to 50% of the gross income of a motion picture. This can be quite important and it does not require a great deal of details. The distributor should be aware of the different requirements of the foreign market when he makes a film or purchases a film. Foreign markets like a great deal of action with very little dialogue. The motion picture should be constructed in

AWARD/CONTRACT

1. CONTRACT (Proc. Inst. Ident.) NO.	2. EFFECTIVE DATE	3. REQUISITION/PURCHASE REQUEST/PROJECT NO.	4. CERTIFIED FOR NATIONAL DEFENSE UNDER BDSA REG. 2 AND/OR DMS REG. 1.
N66398-78-C-0044	14 APR		RATING

3. ISSUED BY   CODE [ ]

BUREAU OF NAVAL PERSONNEL
DEPARTMENT OF THE NAVY
WASHINGTON, D.C. 20370

6. ADMINISTERED BY *(If other than block 5)*   CODE [ ]

NAVY MOTION PICTURE SERVICE
BUILDING 311 FLUSHING AVENUE
BROOKLYN, NEW YORK 11251

7. DELIVERY
☒ FOB DESTINATION
☐ OTHER *(See below)*

3. CONTRACTOR NAME AND ADDRESS   CODE [ ]

FILMS INTERNATIONAL
731 NORTH LABREA AVENUE
HOLLYWOOD, CA 90038

(Street, city, county, State, and ZIP code.)

FACILITY CODE [ ]

9. DISCOUNT FOR PROMPT PAYMENT

N/A

10. SUBMIT INVOICES *(4 copies unless otherwise specified)* **TO ADDRESS SHOWN IN BLOCK** 6

11. SHIP TO/MARK FOR   CODE [ ]

NAVY MOTION PICTURE SERVICE
BUILDING 311 FLUSHING AVENUE
BROOKLYN, NEW YORK 11251

12. PAYMENT WILL BE MADE BY   CODE [ ]

FLEET ACCOUNTING & DISBURSING CENTER, ATLANTIC
NORFOLK, VA 23511

13. THIS PROCUREMENT WAS ☐ ADVERTISED, ☒ NEGOTIATED, PURSUANT TO:
☒ 10 U.S.C. 2304 (a)( ) 0
☐ 41 U.S.C. 252 (c)( )

14. ACCOUNTING AND APPROPRIATION DATA

SEE CONTINUATION SHEET

15. ITEM NO	16. SUPPLIES/SERVICES	17. QUANTITY	18. UNIT	19. UNIT PRICE	20. AMOUNT
	This Contract N66398-78-C-0044 consists of the Title and Signature Page (GSA Standard Form 26), continuation sheet SF 36 and Appendix A.				

1.	16mm sound on film prints of The Feature motion picture ____________ (STANDARD PICTURE PROCESS) COLOR, PRINTED ON ESTAR BASE FILM STOCK. SPECIFICATION a. The forty-five (45) 16mm prints of ____________ shall be leased to the Navy for a rental period of thirty-six (36) months from the date of delivery of such prints	45			

21. TOTAL AMOUNT OF CONTRACT $

CONTRACTING OFFICER WILL COMPLETE BLOCK 22 OR 26 AS APPLICABLE

22. ☐ CONTRACTOR'S NEGOTIATED AGREEMENT (*Contractor is required to sign this document and return* 3 *copies to issuing office.*) Contractor agrees to furnish and deliver all items or perform all the services set forth or otherwise identified above and on any continuation sheets for the consideration stated herein. The rights and obligations of the parties to this contract shall be subject to and governed by the following documents: (a) this award/contract, (b) the solicitation, if any, and (c) such provisions, representations, certifications, and specifications, as are attached or incorporated by reference herein. (*Attachments are listed herein.*)

26. ☐ AWARD (*Contractor is not required to sign this document.*) Your offer on Solicitation Number ____________, including the additions or changes made by you which additions or changes are set forth in full above, is hereby accepted as to the items listed above and on any continuation sheets. This award consummates the contract which consists of the following documents: (a) the Government's solicitation and your offer, and (b) this award/contract. No further contractual document is necessary.

23. NAME OF CONTRACTOR BY ______ FILMS INTERNATIONAL [signature] (Signature of person authorized to sign)	27. UNITED STATES OF AMERICA BY ____________ (Signature of Contracting Officer)

24. NAME AND TITLE OF SIGNER (*Type or print*) Shel Haims - Pres	25. DATE SIGNED	28. NAME OF CONTRACTING OFFICER (*Type or print*)	29. DATE SIGNED

26-105

U. S. GOVERNMENT PRINTING OFFICE

Fig. 13-3. An award contract from the Bureau of Naval Personnel. The name and price of the film have been deleted.

STANDARD FORM 36, JULY 1966 GENERAL SERVICES ADMINISTRATION FED. PROC. REG. (41 CFR) 1-16.101	CONTINUATION SHEET	REF. NO. OF DOC. BEING CONT'D. N66398-78-C-0044		PAGE 2	OF 2

NAME OF OFFEROR OR CONTRACTOR

FILMS INTERNATIONAL

ITEM NO.	SUPPLIES/SERVICES	QUANTITY	UNIT	UNIT PRICE	AMOUNT
	and the Navy shall have an additional period of six months thereafter to effect the return of such prints to the Contractor at its office or designated exchange or laboratory in New York City.				
	b. The Navy as lessee will endeavor to return to the Contractor upon expiration the leasing period every positive print furnished hereunder. However, the Navy does not insure their return. In the case of loss or accidental destruction of prints, the Navy Motion Picture Service will issue a tracer for prints not returned or accounted for. If such tracer fails to produce or account for the missing prints, the Navy Motion Picture Service will issue a certificate of presumed loss which shall release the Navy from any further accounting for such missing prints. If such missing prints turn up in Navy custody at a later date, the Navy will return them to Contractor at such time. The Navy shall not be responsible for the condition of returned prints.				

c. All 16mm Prints shall be delivered
mounted on plastic hubs containing no more
than 1600 ft. per reel.

d. The 16mm prints furnished hereunder
shall with respect to sound be produced
from a re-recorded sound track negative and
shall be printed in the Standard emulsion
position.

e. The prints to be delivered FOB Navy
Motion Picture Service, Brooklyn, NY or
contractors exchange or laboratory New York,
New York with 30 days after receipt of order.

ACCOUNTING AND APPROPRIATION DATA

17X6875.1250-000-46011-0-000189-2D-000000-000010100189

Fig. 13-3. An award contract from the Bureau of Naval Personnel. The name and price of the film have been deleted (continued from page 204).

STANDARD FORM 33, NOV. 1969 GENERAL SERVICES ADMINISTRATION FED. PROC. REG. (41 CFR) 1-16.101	SOLICITATION, OFFER, AND AWARD	3. CERTIFIED FOR NATIONAL DEFENSE UNDER BDSA REG. 2 AND/OR DMS REG. 1. RATING;		1. PAGE	OF

1. CONTRACT *(Proc. Inst. Ident.)* **NO.**

2. SOLICITATION NO.
RFP#MDA902-78-RFQ-
☐ ADVERTISED *(IFB)* ☒ NEGOTIATED *(RFP)* 0174

5. DATE ISSUED 78 Apr 14

4. REQUISITION/PURCHASE REQUEST NO.
4-50. (V-64)
(V-65)

7. ISSUED BY **CODE**
American Forces Radio & Television
Service
1016 N. McCadden Place
Los Angeles, CA 90038

8. ADDRESS OFFER TO *(If other than Block 7)*

SOLICITATION

9. Sealed offers in original and __1__ copies for furnishing the supplies or services described in the Schedule will be received at the place specified in block 8, OR IF HAND-CARRIED, IN THE DEPOSITARY LOCATED IN _____. If this is an advertised solicitation, offers will be publicly opened at that until _____

(Time, Zone, and Date)

time. CAUTION—LATE OFFERS. See par. 8 of Solicitation Instructions and Conditions.
All offers are subject to the following:
1. The attached Solicitation Instructions and Conditions, SF 33-A.
2. The General Provisions, SF 32 _____ edition, which is attached or incorporated herein by reference.

3. The Schedule included below and/or attached hereto.
4. Such other provisions, representations, certifications, and specifications as are attached or incorporated herein by reference. (Attachments are listed in the Schedule.)

FOR INFORMATION CALL *(Name and Telephone No.) (No collect calls):*

TABLE OF CONTENTS

		The following checked sections are contained in the contract.				
(X)	Sec.		Page	(X)	Sec.		Page
	A	Cover Sheet			G	Preservation/Packaging/Packing	
		PART I - GENERAL INSTRUCTIONS			H	Deliveries or Performance	
	B	Contract Form and Representations, Certifications, and Other Statements of Offeror.			I	Inspection and Acceptance	
					J	Special Provisions	
					K	Contract Administration Data	
	C	Instructions, Conditions, and Notices to Offerers.				PART III - GENERAL PROVISIONS	
					L	General Provisions	
	D	Evaluation and Award Factors				PART IV - LIST OF DOCUMENTS AND ATTACHMENTS	
		PART II - THE SCHEDULE					
	E	Supplies/Services and Prices			M	List of Documents and Attachments	
	F	Description/Specifications					

OFFER *(NOTE: Reverse Must Also Be Fully Completed by Offeror)*

206

In compliance with the above, the undersigned offers and agrees, if this offer is accepted within _____ calendar days (60 calendar days unless a different period is inserted by the offeror) from the date for receipt of offers specified above, to furnish any or all items upon which prices are offered, at the price set opposite each item, delivered at the designated point(s), within the time specified in the Schedule.

16. DISCOUNT FOR PROMPT PAYMENT (See Par. 9 on SF 33-A)				
_____ % 10 CALENDAR DAYS;	_____ % 20 CALENDAR DAYS;	_____ % 30 CALENDAR DAYS;	_____ % _____	_____ CALENDAR DAYS.

17. OFFEROR NAME & ADDRESS	CODE		FACILITY CODE	18. NAME AND TITLE OF PERSON AUTHORIZED TO SIGN OFFER (Type or Print)
Enterprises Avenue of the Americas New York, New York 10036				

(Street, city, county, state, & ZIP Code)

Area Code and Telephone No.:

☐ Check If Remittance Address Is Different From Above—Enter Such Address In Schedule.

19. SIGNATURE	20. OFFER DATE

AWARD (To Be Completed By Government)

21. ACCEPTED AS TO ITEMS NUMBERED	22. AMOUNT	23. ACCOUNTING AND APPROPRIATION DATA
		5130

24. SUBMIT INVOICES (4 copies unless otherwise specified) TO ADDRESS SHOWN IN BLOCK	25. NEGOTIATED PURSUANT TO	☒ 10 U.S.C. 2304(a) 10 ☐ 41 U.S.C. 252(c) ( )

26. ADMINISTERED BY (If other than block 7)	CODE	27. PAYMENT WILL BE MADE BY	CODE
		Finance and Accounting Office Fort Ord, CA 93941	

28. NAME OF CONTRACTING OFFICER (Type or Print)	29. UNITED STATES OF AMERICA	30. AWARD DATE
BEVERLY K. FOTIADES	BY: _____ (Signature of Contracting Officer)	

Award will be made on this form, or on Standard Form 26, or by other official written notice.

33-128

Fig. 13-4. A sample Armed Forces Radio and Television Service Award.

FILM RECEIVING REPORT

FROM: .... `Enterprises`
...............Avenue of the Americas
.............New York, New York 10036......

DATE: ....

DEL: By 1 Jul 1978

V-64 Provide (1) Color Print and Transfer Rights to MOVIES (SEE BELOW)

PROGRAM	PROG. NO.	MASTER NO.	QUANTITY		REMARKS
			PRINTS	REELS	
Approx. 105-Min MOVIES					
1.					
2.					
3.					
4.					
5.					
6.					
7.					

8.

Approx. 120-Min MOVIE:

9.

CHECKED BY: ....

ORIGINAL COPY TO FILM PROCESSING
PINK COPY TO TV PROGRAM BRANCH
CANARY COPY TO P&C OFFICER

AFRTS Form 1
26 Jun 73

AFLC/MAF

Fig. 13-4. A sample Armed Forces Radio and Television Service Award (continued from page 208).

A G R E E M E N T

AGREEMENT made this _____ day of _____ 19___ , by and between
_____ having its principal office at
_____ U.S.A., and hereinafter referred to

as "LICENSOR," and _____ hereinafter referred to as "LICENSEE."
having its principal office at _____

W I T N E S S E T H:

1. Licensor hereby grants to Licensee, and Licensee hereby accepts from
Licensor, upon the terms and conditions of this Agreement, the sole and exclusive License to exhibit and distribute to exhibitors, for exhibition for
theatrical and non-theatrical purposes only, for a period of _____ years
from date hereof, the following motion picture (s) to wit:

in the following territory only: _____

2. Licensee agrees to pay to Licensor, in consideration of the License herein mentioned the sum of: _____

payable as follows: _____

3. When ordered by Licensee, Licensor agrees to supply Licensee with such 35mm prints, 35mm trailers, advertising matter and accessories for such motion picture (s) as Licensor may have in stock or can secure from stock, all in the English language. All cost of these materials shall be for the account of Licensee, ex-laboratory. All materials will be supplied f.o.b. U.S. laboratory, or accessory supplier. Costs of all prints, trailers and advertising, will be supplied at Licensor's usual rates charged for said materials.

4. It is agreed that legal title in all prints, advertising matter and accessories delivered hereunder shall remain in the Licensor at all times, subject to the right of Licensee to the use thereof, in accordance and subject to the terms of this Agreement.

Fig. 13-5. A typical foreign sales agreement between the buyer and the seller.

The Licensee agrees that it will not exhibit or perform, or permit to be exhibited or performed, either directly or indirectly, in any territory other than set forth in Article 1 of this Agreement, any prints of said motion pictures in its possession or under its control; that it will not part with the right of possession of said prints or any part thereof or advertising matter or accessories, except in accordance with the condition of this Agreement; that if said prints or any part thereof furnished to said Licensee are stolen or destroyed, it will notify the Licensor immediately by registered letter, postage prepaid, and will use all reasonable endeavors at its own expense to recover the same, and will promptly furnish to Licensor full affidavits establishing such theft or destruction; that it will furnish said Licensor within twenty-four hours of such a request, therefor, with full and accurate information of the locations at any stated times of any prints of said motion pictures furnished by said Licensor which said Licensee may have in its possession or under its control; that at the expiration of the time specified in Article 1 of this Agreement or sooner termination thereof; it will return all prints and all parts thereof to said Licensor at Licensee's expense, at the Licensor's office located in Los Angeles; that in the event Licensee does not promptly return to Licensor all prints at the expiration of such period specified, the Licensor may seize the same wherever found without recourse or liability to the Licensor, and all charges and cost to secure said prints shall be paid by Licensee.

Licensee agrees at all times to keep said prints furnished by Licensor in good condition in order to give proper projections and performances thereof, and will not remove or permit the removal of the name of the Licensor, producer, director, author or principal actors, or any other designation or credit from the prints, advertising matter or accessories supplied hereunder, without the written consent of the Licensor. Licensee agrees that all newspaper advertising and publicity matter shall strictly conform both as to the form of the announcement, as well as to the relative size of the type, to that contained in the advertising matter and accessories furnished by Licensor with respect to each such respective motion picture. The Licensee further agrees to include in the agreement made with each exhibitor in the territory herein embraced, a provision containing the substance of this article.

Licensee agrees that it will not lease, purchase or accept any prints, advertising matter or accessories of the Motion Picture (s) embraced within the terms of this Agreement from any person, firm, or corporation other than the Licensor.

5. It is understood and agreed that Licensee is not the representative of the Licensor in any manner whatsoever, and Licensee agrees not to so hold out, either by advertising or otherwise to the public or to any party whomsoever, and that Licensor shall not be liable for or bound by any representation, act or omission whatsoever of Licensee.

It is further expressly understood and agreed that this Agreement in no wise constitutes a partnership between the parties hereto, or a joint venture between the parties hereto.

Fig. 13-5. A typical foreign sales agreement between the buyer and the seller (continued from page 212).

6. It is agreed that the Licensor shall not be liable for any failure to deliver, or delay in delivery of prints, advertising matter or accessories, or for any damage or loss occasioned by wars, delays of transportation, force majeure, acts of God, or any other causes beyond its control. Licensor shall have the right and option to terminate this Agreement as to all or any pictures affected thereby, or to substitute a picture of equal standard to the picture or pictures which Licensor was unable to deliver. It is also agreed that if Licensor shall, for any reason, fail to manufacture any motion picture embraced herein, the Licensor shall be freed from the obligation to make delivery thereof, and such picture shall be deemed excluded from this Agreement with the same effect as if it had never been embraced herein.

7. Where a series of pictures are to be delivered, pursuant to the terms of this Agreement, a default in any of the payments herein provided, including any royalty payment or any payment for negatives, prints, advertising matter, or accessories, shall relieve the Licensor of the necessity of delivery or tendering delivery of any negatives, prints, advertising matter or accessories of any preceding or succeeding pictures. Notwithstanding the fact that the Licensor shall be relieved of delivery or tendering delivery of any prints, advertising matter or accessories, the Licensee shall remain and continue fully liable for the full payment of the entire balance of the monies payable as royalties under this Agreement with respect to the balance of the pictures; and it is expressly agreed that the amount of all royalties agreed to be paid on the balance of the Pictures shall be deemed to be the damages sustained by the Licensor by reason of such default, and Licensor shall have the right to collect and enforce the collection from the Licensee of such entire balance as and for its damages hereunder.

A waiver of any breach shall not be construed as a continuing waiver for a similar breach, and such waiver shall be effective only when made in writing.

8. It is agreed by and between the parties hereto that all questions arising hereunder shall be interpreted and governed under and by the laws of the State of California of the United States of America.

9. The rights of Licensee under this Agreement are dependent and conditional upon the due and faithful performance by the Licensee of each of the terms and conditions herein contained, all of which are hereby agreed upon as being the essence of this Agreement. In case of Licensee's default in the due performance of any of the terms or conditions on its parts to be performed, Licensor may at its election mail or cable a notice to Licensee specifying the nature of the default complained of, and in case said default shall not be rectified within ten (10) days after the cabling of such notice, or if Licensee shall be adjudged a bankrupt, or should a receiver, trustee, or liquidator of the Licensee's property be appointed by any court or other legal authority, then and in any such event, all the rights granted hereunder to Licensee shall terminate and revert to Licensor but without prejudice to and in addition to and all rights to compensation or damage or to any cause of action which the Licensor may have against the Licensee, and Licensor shall have the right to keep and retain absolutely the deposit and any other payments theretofore made to Licensor, as and for Licensor's partial liquidated damages and on account of any claims the Licensor may then have or thereafter have against the Licensee. Moreover, in case of

Fig. 13-5. A typical sales agreement between the buyer and the seller (continued from page 214).

any such default as aforesaid and the failure to rectify the same within the period above provided, all the royalties fixed herein as payable upon all the remaining motion picture (s) deliverable hereunder from and after the date of such default, shall forthwith become due and owing to Licensor from Licensee with the same full force and effect as if all such motion picture (s) had actually been delivered to Licensee in accordance with the terms of this Agreement.

10.   All royalty prices quoted in this contract are net of any government withholding taxes imposed on either Licensor or Licensee. It is specifically agreed that Licensee will be responsible for payment of all taxes imposed by the governments of the territories covered under the terms of this contract, or by the government where the licensee's company is located.

11.   This Agreement is binding upon the parties hereto, their heirs, executors, administrators, successors and assigns.

12.   CENSOR CLAUSE: If the film (s) is banned or cuts made which will render the film (s) unsuitable, Licensor agrees to substitute another film(s) of equal value, subject to Licensee's approval or refund the royalty in full, providing Licensee meets the two following qualifications: (1) Licensee will advise Licensor of banning of film(s) within sixty (60) days from receipt of print(s). Said notification must be accompanied by an official document from the censor board substantiating censor refusal. (2) Licensee must return at Licensee's expense, all prints, trailers and advertising material to Licensor

After receipt of said materials, Licensor will refund the royalty and upon sale of material returned, Licensor will pay or credit to Licensee the proceeds of said sale, (original cost of materials, less import expenses and other direct sales costs).

IN WITNESS WHEREOF, the parties hereto have caused this Agreement to be duly executed the day and year first above written.

By: _____ (LICENSOR)

By: _____ (LICENSEE)

Fig. 13-5. A typical foreign sales agreement between the buyer and the seller (continued from page 216).

REPRESENTATION AGREEMENT

THIS AGREEMENT, made and entered into this _____ day of _____ 19___ by and between _____ located at _____ hereinafter referred to as "Owner", and _____ located at _____ hereinafter referred to as "Representative".

W I T N E S S E T H

WHEREAS, Owner, hereby, warrants that it is the exclusive one hundred percent (100%) Owner of the motion picture(s) entitled:

(hereinafter individually and collectively "the Picture"), and has the right to grant the distribution rights hereinafter mentioned, and is desirous of granting said rights to buyers through Representative upon the terms and conditions hereinafter stated; and

WHEREAS, Owner represents and warrants that the Picture at the time of delivery shall be copyrighted; Owner has the right to enter into this Agreement and grant exclusively to Representative any and all of the rights set forth in this Agreement; at the time of delivery of the Picture shall be free of all outstanding claims, liens or encumberances of any nature which might in any way interfere with the rights granted to Representative hereunder; Owner has not and shall not in the future do, authorize, allow or cause to be done any act (or omission) which has or might interfere with the rights granted to Representative hereunder; Owner has all of the underlying rights in and to the

Picture; the credits as set forth in the Picture and all advertising materials delivered to Representative are correct and complete, and Representative shall not be responsible for any failure to accord any credit not so supplied; neither the distribution, sale or other exploitation of the Picture nor any par thereof (including the music and sound synchronized therewith) nor the exercise by Representative (or any party authorized by Representative) of any of the rights granted to Representative hereunder will violate or infringe upon the trademark, trade name, copyright, contract, literary, dramatic, musical, rights of privacy, or any other rights of any party or be in any manner defamatory of any party; and,

WHEREAS, Representative is engaged in the business of selling motion pictures and is desirous of obtaining the representation rights to the Picture, upon the terms and conditions herein stated;

NOW THEREFORE, for the various considerations herein contained it is hereby agreed between the parties hereto as follows:

1. Owner grants to Representative and Representative hereby accepts from Owner, upon the terms and conditions and provisions stated in this Agreement, the sole and exclusive right to represent Owner and market the Picture and the prints thereof, for theatrical, non-theatrical and videotape exhibition in theatres, hotels, or otherwise, and television purposes and uses, in all gauges and/or processes now in existence, or which may hereafter be discovered, for a period commencing at the date hereof up to and including throughout the entire world and Canada.

Fig. 13-6. An agreement between a distributor and a foreign sales agent.

219

2. Representative has the right to effect sales for a period of up to ten (10) years at any time during the life of the Agreement.

Owner agrees to deliver to Representative for each motion picture comprising the Picture prior to _____, the following:

(A) Laboratory Access Letter signed by Owner and Laboratory per sample attached as Exhibit "A".

(B) Letter to Accessory Service to honor all accessory orders from Representative at wholesale prices.

(C) One print and one trailer in 35mm of the Picture, to be delivered to Representative at its office set forth above.

(D) Sample of all publicity and advertising materials available.

(E) One set of at least 100 different color transparencies depicting scenes from the Picture.

(F) Three copies of the music cue sheet of the Picture.

(G) No less than 10 copies of the English dialogue list of the Picture and trailer.

(H) Quarter inch tape of music and effects tracks of feature and trailer.

(I) No less than 100 pressbooks.

(J) One textless, clear title background 35mm negative or internegative of the trailer and the main and end title sections of the Picture.

3. Owner agrees to make the negative or internegative of the Picture available to Representative at all times as needed for shipment to those countries which require the loan of the negative.

4. The term "gross receipts" as used herein shall mean all sums of money paid to Representative by any distributors or buyers (either on a flat sum payment or percentage basis) for the use and exhibition of the Picture. The term "net receipts" as used herein shall mean all gross receipts less Representative's costs of promotional advertising, freight, and forwarding costs for screening prints, and screening charges, direct sales costs, any unreimbursed direct out-of-pocket expenses incurred by Representative in connection with the sale or other exploitation of Picture, and any other deductions permitted by this Agreement. However, if Representative uses any sub-distributors in connection with the sale or other exploitation of the Picture, Representative shall be wholly responsible for the payment of such sub-distributor's fees out of Representative's share of the net receipts (as set forth below), and such sub-distributor's fees shall not be deductible from gross receipts in the calculation of net receipts.

Representative shall pay for all new positive release prints of the Picture ordered by it from any laboratory from the date of this Agreement, for advertising accessories ordered by it from the date of this Agreement, and for the costs of shipping such release prints and advertising accessories to distributors or buyers, except that to the extent Representative is not reimbursed for the costs thereof by such distributors or buyers, such unreimbursed costs shall be deducted by Representative from gross receipts in the calculation of net receipts. Owner acknowledges that Representative shall be entitled to all monies paid to Representative by such buyers or distributors for any prints or advertising accessories (and shipping costs therefor) furnished by Representative to such buyers or distributors in connection with the Picture, and such monies shall be excluded from gross receipts. Owner acknowledges that Representative shall be entitled to charge a reasonable handling fee in

Fig. 13-6. An agreement between a distributor and a foreign sales agent (continued from page 220).

connection with such release prints and advertising accessories, but Representative hereby warrants and represents to Owner that the price charged by Representative for such release prints and advertising accessories shall be comparable to prices charged by other representatives and distributors for similar items in similar markets.

Net receipts shall be divided _____ percent (___ %) to Owner, and _____ percent (___ %) to Representative.

5. Representative hereby agrees to provide and submit to Owner with respect to the exploitation of the Picture, monthly statements and reports commencing on _____ and continuing to _____, quarterly reports for two (2) years and semi-annual reports thereafter, for as long as monies are being received by Representative in connection with the Picture. Said statements and reports shall be accompanied by payment to Owner of all su due to Owner under this Agreement. Said reports shall be submitted and delivered not later than the twentieth of each month after the end of each accounting period, commencing on _____.

Representative shall keep and maintain separate books of account of all gross receipts received from the distribution or other exploitation of the Picture, and all costs, expenses or other deductions from such gross receipts. During Representative's normal business hours, and upon reasonable prior writt notice to Representative, Owner may cause any Certified Public Accountant (dul licensed in the State of California) to inspect the above-described books of account and records of Representative pertaining to the Picture for audit purposes, at Owner's expense. Owner agrees that such audit shall not be made mor than once during any calendar year. Unless first objected to by a writing specifying the reasons for such objection in reasonable detail, any report or statement of account by Representative to Owner hereunder shall become in-contestible by Owner two (2) years from the date of rendering hereof.

6. INDEMNITY: Owner shall defend, indemnify, and save Representative and its assigns wholly harmless against any loss, claim, damages, judgments and other costs or expenses (including reasonable attorney's fees) incurred by Representative or its assigns arising out of or connected with any breach or alleged breach of any warranty or representation made by Owner hereunder. In the event of any claim which if true would be such a breach, Representative may withhold a reasonable amount of monies otherwise payable to Owner here-under, and may reimburse itself for any such costs incurred in connection therewith.

7. All written notices required hereunder shall be sent to the respective parties by mail, postage prepaid, telegram or cable as follows:

<u>TO OWNER:</u>

<u>TO REPRESENTATIVE:</u>

or to such other address as may be communicated to the other party by written notice.

Fig. 13-6. An agreement between a distributor and a foreign sales agent (continued from page 222).

223

8. Representative shall have sole discretion in the exercise of the rights, licenses and privileges hereunder and shall have the right to decide when, where, how and on what basis, and to what extent it will exploit the rights hereunder. Representative makes no warranties, and no warranties shall be implied that the efforts of the Representative with respect to the exploitation of the rights granted to it hereunder shall result in any net receipts with respect to the Picture. Representative may make any changes with respect to the Picture that it (in its sole discretion) deems necessary or appropriate in connection with the exploitation thereof, including, but not limited to, changes required for television exhibition, compliance with local censorship laws, obtaining a more favorable rating regarding the scope of the audience, or in connection with dubbing, sub-titles or otherwise concerning foreign language distribution of the Picture.

9. This Agreement constitutes the entire understanding of the parties, and may be altered only by a written instrument signed by all of the parties hereto. This Agreement is and shall be binding upon the parties hereto and their respective assigns and successors in interest. California law shall govern this Agreement.

10. The relationship of the parties hereto is that of independent contractor and in no manner shall be construed as creating a joint venture and/or employee status.

224

11. In the event REPRESENTATIVE does not effect sales totalling within one (1) year of this Agreement, on the film, OWNER reserves the right to cancel the Agreement by notifying REPRESENTATIVE in writing. OWNER, will, however, honor all contracts obtained by REPRESENTATIVE.

IN WITNESS WHEREOF, the parties approve and enter into this Agreement on the date and year first written above.

BY: _____
       "OWNER"

BY: _____
       "REPRESENTATIVE"

Fig. 13-6. An agreement between a distributor and a foreign sales agent (continued from page 224).

Table 13-2. Foreign Countries Purchasing American Films.

TERRITORY	MAX. EST. GROSS	MIN. EST. GROSS
Argentina - Uraguay - Paraguay	$ 8000.	$ 4000.
Australia..................................	10000.	5000.
Belgium..................................	3000.	1500.
Bermuda..................................	3000.	1500.
Brazil..................................	6000.	3000.
British West Africa....................	6000.	3000.
Burma..................................	4000.	2000.
Central America........................	2000.	1000.
Canada..................................	10000.	5000.
Ceylon..................................	4000.	2000.
Chile..................................	2000.	1000.
Colombia..................................	3000.	1500.
Denmark..................................	4000.	2000.
East Africa..................................	5000.	2500.
Egypt..................................	5000.	2500.
England..................................	12000.	6000.
Fiji Islands - New Zealand..........	5000.	2500.
Finland..................................	4000.	2000.
France..................................	15000.	7500.
Germany and Austria..............	15000.	7500.
Greece..................................	6000.	3000.
Holland..................................	4000.	2000.
Hong Kong/Macao....................	6000.	3000.
India..................................	10000.	5000.
Indonesia..................................	5000.	2500.
Iran..................................	4000.	2000.
Israel..................................	6000.	3000.
Italy..................................	15000.	7500.
Jamaica..................................	3000.	1500.
Japan..................................	20000.	10000.
Korea..................................	6000.	3000.
Malaysia..................................	5000.	2500.
Mexico..................................	6000.	3000.
Middle East..................................	5000.	2500.
Norway..................................	4000.	2000.
Pakistan..................................	6000.	3000.
Peru - Bolivia - Ecuador..........	3000.	1500.
Philippines..................................	8000.	4000.
Portugal..................................	5000.	2500.
Puerto Rico..................................	6000.	3000.
Singapore..................................	2000.	1000.
South Africa..................................	8000.	4000.
Spain..................................	15000.	7500.
Sweden..................................	5000.	2500.
Switzerland..................................	3000.	1500.
Taiwan (Formosa)....................	5000.	2500.
Thailand..................................	5000.	2500.
Trinidad..................................	3000.	1500.
Turkey..................................	4000.	2000.
Venezuela..................................	6000.	3000.
Viet-Nam..................................	3000.	1500.
Yugoslavia..................................	6000.	3000.
TOTALS..................................	$324000.	$162000.

Table 13-3. Areas of the World Purchasing American Films.

EUROPE	ASIA
Belgium	Burma
Denmark	Ceylon
England	Hong Kong and Macao
Finland	India
France	Indonesia
Germany-Austria	Japan
Greece	Korea
Holland	Malaysia
Italy	Pakistan
Norway	Philippines
Portugal	Taiwan
Spain	Thailand
Sweden	Viet-Nam
Switzerland	Singapore
Yugoslavia	Australia
	Fiji Islands and New Zealand

LATIN AMERICA	MIDDLE EAST
Argentina-Uraguay-Paraguay	West Africa
Brazil	East Africa
Central America	South Africa
Chile	Egypt
Columbia	Iran
Mexico	Israel
Peru-Bolivia-Ecuador	Middle East
Venezuela	Turkey
Bermuda	
Jamaica	
Puerto Rico	
Trinidad	

*There are instances where some smaller countries not listed above will purchase motion pictures.

such a way that a native of India watching the film would understand the contents of the film and not know a word of the dialogue. The action would lead him through the entire plot. Many distributors make the mistake of liking a film due to the local color and dialogue but this is lost sometimes on the foreign market. If too much sub-titling is necessary or dubbing, the audience loses the feel of the motion picture.

For information and edification, Tables 13-2 and 13-3 list the countries that purchase American films. Also listed is the maximum gross and the minimum gross of the amount of U.S. dollars they will pay.

The prices established are based on a normal motion picture that has relative value and has played in the United States with a modest amount of success. The film would not be a block-buster and in all probability it would be distributed by an independent motion picture distributor. The actors will not have much name value but the film will have international appeal. These lists of countries and prices should only be used as a guide since each film must be sold on its own merit. Also, these prices do not project possible future inflation.

However, even though a film may do rather poorly in the United States, it does not necessarily mean that it will do poorly on the International Market. Conversely, foreign films which do well abroad may do poorly in the United States.

INTERNATIONAL MOTION PICTURE ACCOUNTING

All foreign motion picture sales are made to a buyer on an agreed length of time. Usually, a five year term is normal. However, it can be any length of time if so agreed and specified in the foreign sales agreement.

After the expiration of the agreed upon term, the motion picture rights revert back to the distributor. If the distribution agreement is no longer in force with the producer, then the motion picture rights revert to the producer.

All accounting procedures on foreign sales will be the same as those outlined in chapter 10—Accounting and Distribution Control. Again, the approval of sales are under the sales manager's jurisdiction. Copies of the foreign agreement should be sent to the sales manager and to the master control division. This will be the responsibility of the accounts receivable department. Additionally, the booking and control clerk must be aware of the sale. If necessary, this clerk must prepare the shipment of prints and accessories as required by the letter of credit.

There are two forms for internal accounting of the distribution company (Figs. 13-7 and 13-8). One form is for the accounting for the individual motion picture and is entitled *INTERNATIONAL MOTION PICTURE SALES* (Fig. 13-7). The form is broken down as follows:

Area and country: List the geographical location and country purchasing film

Motion Picture and length of license: List motion picture and time period.

CRICKET FILM PRODUCTIONS, INC.

INTERNATIONAL MOTION PICTURE SALES FORM

FOREIGN AREA: _____

FOREIGN COUNTRY: _____

TITLE OF MOTION PICTURE: _____

LENGTH OF TIME OF LICENSE: _____

NAME AND ADDRESS OF FOREIGN BUYER	FOREIGN SALES REPRESENTATIVE	GROSS AMOUNT OF FOREIGN SALE	LESS REPRESENTATIVE SALES COMMISSION	NET INCOME TO DISTRIBUTOR	REMARKS

Fig. 13-7. An international motion picture sales form.

229

Name and address of purchaser: List name and address of buyer.

Sales representative: List representative if any.

Gross sales price: List the gross sales price which picture sold for.

Less sales commission: List sales commission, if any.

Net income to Distribution Co.: Show net income received from foreign sale.

Remarks: List all pertinent remarks applicable to the sale.

The other form (Fig. 13-8) is basically the same as the motion picture sale except that the filing is under the purchaser rather than under the motion picture. In this form one purchaser can be the buyer of several films and these films are so listed.

NON-THEATRICAL INCOME

Non-theatrical selling is a highly specialized sales art form. The key to this market is in packaging and selling. Most motion picture distributors are not aware of the potential income that can be realized from the non-theatrical sales of a motion picture. However, the sales campaign requires extensive mailing lists, a thorough knowledge of these markets and a great deal of personal contact.

Student interest in films is growing and percentage deals with colleges and universities sometimes outgross motion picture theatre rentals. This is in spite of the fact that non-theatrical exhibition forbids public advertising in such media as commercial radio stations, television stations and commercial newspapers and magazines.

Rentals or outright sales vary depending on the motion picture offered. Motion picture distributors usually get their money up front, unlike theatrical motion picture distribution.

Non-theatrical films consist of a wide spectrum of subjects geared to suit the particular tastes of all audiences. They are usually broken down into seven categories:

■ Drama
■ Musicals
■ Comedies
■ Action and adventure
■ Children's films
■ Educational films
■ Science and health films

There are two basic methods to reach and create sales for non-theatrical films.

CRICKET FILM PRODUCTIONS INC.

INTERNATIONAL PURCHASER CONTROL FORM

FOREIGN AREA: _____

FOREIGN COUNTRY: _____

NAME AND ADDRESS OF FOREIGN BUYER

TITLE OF MOTION PICTURE	DATE SOLD	LENGTH OF TIME OF LICENSE	FOREIGN SALES REPRESENTATIVE	GROSS AMOUNT OF FOREIGN SALE	LESS REPRESENTATIVE SALES COMMISSION	NET INCOME DISTRIBUTOR	REMARKS

Fig. 13-8. An international purchaser control form.

Direct Contact

Direct contact is one method of creating sales for non-theatrical films. This direct contact includes: Personal visits to organizations and individuals, the telephone approach and physical showings, such as at film festivals, etc.

Indirect Contact

A second approach is through indirect contact which includes: mailing brochures to customers and advertising of services and promotions.

Generally, the indirect contact is used on non-theatrical sales. Normally, non-theatrical sales are not made in 35 mm film. They are usually used as: 16 mm films, 8 mm films and videotapes.

There are many surprising outlets for these non-theatrical films including fund-raising for religious, ethnic groups and business employees. Non-theatrical films are sold or rented to the following:

■ State, county, municipal and federal government agencies.

■ Educational organizations.

■ Schools, including elementary, high schools, colleges and universities.

■ Hotels and resorts.

■ Airlines.

■ Film societies.

■ Museums.

■ Private home showings and collectors.

■ Business and industries.

■ Churches and Synagogues.

■ Hospitals and sanitariums.

■ Ship viewings and seamen's clubs on shore.

■ Trade associations and organizations.

■ Correctional and prison institutions.

All sales are either made on an outright cash basis or on rental agreements. In the case of a rental agreement, the rentee is responsible for the following:

■ Maintaining the print in satisfactory condition.

■ Paying the rental rate.

■ Returning the print.

■ All damages to the print while in the possession of the rentee.

- No advertising commercially on the print.
- Default payment if cancelled by rentee.

Warner Brothers Communications Company is a large distributor of non-theatrical films. Currently, they are exploiting the entertainment of business. They offer over 100 motion pictures to employees of business. The cost of viewing these films is paid for by the company, employee association or sometimes a nominal admission charge.

Many companies are signing up for such films. Most of these companies have large auditoriums in which they show the films over extended periods at lunch hours or on Friday and Saturday nights.

Universal-International Pictures is another major distributor in the field, hitting hard at the educational level.

The motion picture distribution company, in order to complete the marketing of the motion picture, must investigate the potentialities of this lucrative market. It is recommended, however, that the motion picture distributor not attempt to do its own selling in this market, but rather employ a non-theatrical sales company. There are many excellent non-theatrical sales companies who would be more than pleased to evaluate the motion picture and give a written estimate of the potential income which could be derived from the exhibition of the motion picture in the non-theatrical market.

Non-theatrical sales companies have the following expertise:
- They know the market.
- They handle all sales and shipments and take care of print inventories.
- They advance all monies necessary for brochures and prints.
- They are a complete entity in themselves and do not require any outside auditing or control.

In the event the motion picture distributor elects to use the services of the non-theatrical sales company, all sales are to be handled per the standard operating procedures outlined previously.

The booking and control clerk will advise the accounts receivable department, the sales manager and the master control unit of all sales and reports.

AGREEMENT made this____day of_____, by and between_____

_____, a New York corporation, (hereinafter called_____), whose address for all purposes hereunder is _____

_____, a California corporation, (hereinafter called "Producer), whose address for all purposes hereunder is Los Angeles, California.

W I T N E S S E T H:

WHEREAS, Producer is the sole owner of a motion picture sound film presently entitled _____ (hereinafter called "the film"), and _____

WHEREAS, the parties hereto desire that____distribute the film.

NOW THEREFORE, in consideration of the premises and mutual promises herein contained, it is agreed as follows:

FIRST: Promptly upon the execution of this Agreement Producer shall, at its expense, procure and deliver to____for its use and disposition the following materials:

a. A technically satisfactory composite master of the film complete with titles and a technically satisfactory composite answer print taken from said master. Said answer print shall contain a narration and music track combined on a Kodachrome print. If said master and answer print are satisfactory to_____shall purchase the same from Producer at standard laboratory cost, and undertake distribution of the film in accordance with the provisions hereinafter set forth.

b. At least ten (10) still negatives of different scenes contained in the film, each negative to be accompanied by a print thereof.

c. Six (6) copies of the scoring script of the film.

d. Written evidence satisfactory to____that reproduction and performance of all music, if any, contained in the film is free and clear for use in connection with exhibition of the film. Such written evidence shall include the music titles, name of composer, performing artist and copyright owner thereof.

SECOND: Producer shall safely store the original picture and sound track of the film and shall make the same available to____at its request, from time to time, _or the purpose of____obtaining in the future such preprint material therefrom as may deem necessary for continued production of release prints of the film. Producer shall keep said original picture and sound track free and clear of all liens and encumbrances whatsoever and shall procure and bear the cost of such insurance thereon as Producer deems advisable. Preprint material obtained by____under this Article and all release prints of the film ordered by EBF shall be paid for by EBF. Title to and ownership of all preprint material and release prints of the film acquired by____shall be in _____

Fig. 13-9. A sample contract of a non-theatrical sales agreement.

THIRD: Producer, at its own expense, shall incorporate into the film all beginning and end titles as specified and approved in writing by____. The presentation, main and credit titles shall be substantially as follows:

Frame
A
                       Presents

B   (Title of Film)

   Copyright (Year Date) by

       Copyright and all rights of reproduction,
        including by television, reserved.

C   In Collaboration With
             (Name of Collaborator)

              Produced by

FOURTH: Producer does hereby grant unto____and____does hereby accept from Producer the sole, exclusive and unrestricted right, license and privilege to reproduce, exhibit and distribute, or cause to be reproduced, exhibited and distributed, release prints of the film in color and in black and white, in any and all gauges, in any and all versions, and throughout the entire world.

_____may use any part or parts of the film including stills for purposes of promotion and in teachers guides predicated on the film.

FIFTH: In consideration of the rights herein granted to_____ shall pay Producer as follows:

A. A royalty of_____per cent (___) of the net sales price actually received by____from the sale of each release print of the film. "Net sales price" as used herein shall mean gross sales price less dealer's discount (if any) and less all taxes, time-payment charges and transportation expenses which may be included in the gross sales price.

SIXTH: Payment of such royalties as may accrue hereunder to Producer in each yearly calendar quarter shall be made by____on or before thirty (30) days after the close of each such quarter and shall be accompanied by a statement of account showing a computation of such royalties.

Royalty on each print sold shall accrue only after____has actually received payment therefor.____, at its election, however, may compute and pay royalty on the basis of prints shipped and not upon payment actually received. Such election by from time to time shall not be deemed a waiver by____ of its right to thereafter compute or recompute royalty on the basis of payment actually received by

In the event prints or reproduction rights to the film are sold in a country or countries outside of the United States wherein a banking or currency restriction prohibits payment therefor in United States currency, the amount of royalties due there-upon to Producer shall be deposited to the credit of Producer in a depository within such country or countries in accordance with such written instructions as Producer shall give to____, which instructions shall not be contrary to law. ____ shall have no further obligation to Producer regarding any such royalties so deposited. All costs on account of such deposits shall be borne by Producer.

Producer, at its expense, may cause a certified public accountant to audit the account of____relative to distribution of the film, provided that such audit shall be made only at such intervals and at such time convenient to____and not more than once in any six (6) month period.

SEVENTH: In the event Producer has not heretofore secured statutory copyright in and to the film,____is hereby authorized to copyright the film in Producer's name in any and all countries throughout the world. Producer shall hold any and all such copyright heretofore or hereafter secured, including renewal or extension thereof, free of all liens and encumbrances whatsoever for the mutual benefit of the parties hereto as long as this Agreement shall remain in effect. Copyright expenses paid by   on be-half of Producer shall be deducted from the first royalties which may accrue to Producer hereunder.

EIGHTH: ____shall distribute the film in accordance with its usual business practice and shall devote such effort to the distribution thereof as it normally accords to other films which it distributes.____shall solely determine all marketing policies regarding distribution of the film, except____shall not distribute the film at prices less than prices charged by____for films of similar nature and length.

NINTH: Producer represents and warrants unto____. That it has heretofore acquired, or will acquire prior to distribution of the film by____, the exclusive right for the production, reproduction, exhibition and distribution of the film and the right to use all rights, plots, ideas, music and themes upon which the film is based or which are contained therein, and the right to use all matters and things which were used in the production of the film and in the recording thereof, and that the film and all rights granted hereunder to____are free and clear of all royalties, license fees, liens and encumbrances whatsoever, except as may be expressly set forth in this Agreement.

That no part of the film, or the exercise of any right granted to____herein violates or will violate, infringes or will infringe the trade-mark, tradename, copyright or literary, artistic, dramatic, property, performance, or patent right or rights, or any other right of any person, firm or corporation and that the film contains no material defamatory or libelous or otherwise unlawful.

That it has not and shall not at any time grant or attempt to grant to any person, firm or corporation rights of any kind or character, the exercise of which would derogate from or compete with the rights granted to____hereunder, and will not furnish or cause to be furnished to any other person, firm or corporation any photography con-

Fig. 13-9. A sample contract of a non-theatrical sales agreement (continued from page 235).

taining scenes or pictures so similar in appearance and content to the scenes and pictures included in the film that such might reasonably be calculated to give the impression of being scenes or pictures contained in the film.

Producer agrees to protect, defend, indemnify and hold harmless____, its officers or agents, against any and all claims, loss or expense which____its officers or agents, may suffer or incur by reason of any person, firm or corporation alleging, commencing or maintaining any action against____, its officers or agents, and based on any of the matters of warranty hereinabove contained.

TENTH: It is understood that the royalty of____ per cent (__) contained in Article Fifth, paragraph A is____per cent (__) more than____normally pays to other producers, therefore, Producer agrees that____per cent (__) of the amount of royalty which is paid to Producer by virtue of said Article Fifth, paragraph A shall be used by Producer for the purpose of research and experimentation in the field of cinema art.

ELEVENTH: The term of this Agreement is for the period of ten (10) years from the date hereof and shall thereafter be automatically extended for successive five (5) year periods unless and until either party shall give to the other written notice of termination no less than six (6) months prior to the expiration of the initial period of ten years or any five year extension thereof.

Upon termination of this Agreement____shall transfer all preprint material of the film then in its possession to Producer and Producer, at its election, may purchase at laboratory cost any and all release prints of the film then in____possession, all such prints not so purchased may be sold by____and royalty thereon paid all in accordance with the provisions of this Agreement.

TWELFTH: This Agreement shall not be assigned by either party without the written consent of the other. Producer hereby consents to an assignment hereof by to any subsidiary or parent corporation of

THIRTEENTH: This Agreement is the complete agreement between the parties relative to the subject matter hereof, and no modification or addition shall be binding unless in writing and executed in the same manner as this Agreement is executed.

FOURTEENTH: It is understood and agreed that the parties hereto are not partners or joint venturers.

FIFTEENTH: The performance of this Agreement shall in all respects be governed by the laws of the State of____pursuant to which laws this Agreement shall be construed and interpreted.

IN WITNESS WHEREOF, the parties hereto have executed this Agreement in duplicate on the day first above written.

ATTEST: _____   By _____

ATTEST: _____   By _____

Many times non-theatrical sales are like "found money". Most distributors never even dream of the potential income which awaits them.

All non-theatrical distribution contracts are different. The terms the distributor offers are usually lower for the producer than for theatrical films because the non-theatrical distributor must expend more time, money and energy in creating and selling this market. The gross income is naturally lower and the paper work is horrendous. Figure 13-9 is a sample contract of a non-theatrical sales agreement.

Glossary

Advertising and promotion clause of distribution agreement: This clause appears in all distribution agreements. The clause outlines the amount of advertising and promotion expenses which may be incurred by the distributor in distributing the motion picture. The producer must be very aware of these costs and he should make sure that the distribution is made between pre-distribution costs and cooperative advertising with theatres. Basically, all costs are for the account of the producer. If not clarified, it could possibly mean the difference between profit and loss.

American Armed Forces Radio and Television Service (overseas): Located in Hollywood, California, this organization furnishes all Armed Forces with videotaped programs for information and entertainment. They purchase films on sports, religion, variety, drama, feature films, fillers, cartoons and short subjects. Address is as follows:

American Forces Radio and Television Service
1016 N. McCadden Place
Los Angeles, California 90038

Ancillary television: This is a film that comes across on a television set. Films are on videotape and are ¾ inch, ½ inch or disc. They are sold for viewing to hotels and motels, in-home use, hospitals, pay for view-television, subscription television and inflight including planes, boats, passenger liners, freighters, tuna boats, oil tankers and oil derricks.

A **negative:** Much film is exposed in making a film, and an *A* negative is that negative actually used in the edited and completed motion picture. It is the terminology used by picture editors, negative cutters and film laboratories designating film which is spliced together per cut work print. It is timed for color saturation and printed by laboratories alongside motion picture optical tracks to make release prints.

answer print: This is the first print made by the film laboratory using an *A* negative and optical track combined. The answer print means just that...the answer. The producer and the film laboratory see exactly how the timing for the color saturation works as well as opticals. They also know if the optical track is in sync with the film. Many times, more work must be done prior to making release prints from the answer print negative. Probably, the answer print should have been called the trial print.

ASCAP: This is a licensing organization. This means that all music played on radio and/or television is paid a royalty to ASCAP. ASCAP, in turn, pays this royalty to the respective composers and artists. ASCAP means American Society of Composers, Artists and Publishers. Their address is:

American Society of Composers, Artists and Publishers
1 Lincoln Plaza
New York, New York 10023

B **negative:** This is a negative not used in the finished cut negative of the motion picture. Sometimes, this negative—or part of it—is used in the making of trailers and opticals. It is stored in the film laboratory vaults and kept separate from the *A* negative.

BMI: Like ASCAP, this is a performing rights organization (non-profit). They are competitors of ASCAP. They also receive royalities from radio and television plays of music. They pass these royalities on to the composers and artists of the music. BMI means Broadcast Music, Inc. and their address is:

Broadcast Music Inc.,
40 W. 57th Street
New York, New York 10019

box office reports: This means the gross income received by the theatre prior to any deductions for advertising or other costs.

cassettes: This is a system where the film is transferred from film to videotape and placed in cassettes, either ¾ inch or ½ inch. This is potentially a billion-dollar market and usually sales are made outright with the producer receiving a royalty on each cassette sold.

Class L & M: This classification is from The Register of Copyright. It designates the class pertaining to the particular type of copyright. Class L & M refers to motion pictures and motion picture teleplays.

certificate of code rating: This certificate is given to the distributor or producer from The Code and Rating Administration of the Motion Picture Association. It clarifies the designation of the motion picture, i.e. "G" General audiences, "PG" Parental Guidance suggested, "R" Restricted, etc.

combo run: Where two pictures of similar content run together as a double bill. Each film is allocated one-half the income equally. If three pictures run together as a combo, then the income is allocated one-third each.

cooperative advertising: This means that the distributor and the theatre share in the cost of the theatre advertising campaign for a particular playdate. Cooperative advertising is agreed upon prior to the playdate of the motion picture.

CRI: CRI means color reversal intermediate negative. This is the process of going from a negative to a negative. Technically, it means reversal where normally one would go from a negative to a print. The process during reversal is from negative to negative.

cross plugs: These are aids used in the promotion and advertising of the motion picture such as the book from the film, or the music album, or the theme song used extensively in the film. In science-fiction, it could be pictures, images or toys from the film.

Department of the Army and the Air Force: Located in Dallas, Texas, it is the procurement agency for both the Army and the Air Force for purchase and distribution of films. Address is as follows:

Army and Air Force Exchange Service
Film Procurement Branch
Dallas, Texas 75222

Department of the Navy: Located in Brooklyn, New York, it is the procurement agency for the Navy Department for purchase and distribution of films. Address is as follows:

Navy Motion Picture Services
Building 311, Flushing Avenue,
Brooklyn, New York 11251

Director of the Code for Advertising: The name and address is as follows:

Director of the Code of Advertising
Motion Picture Association of America
522 Fifth Avenue
New York, New York 10036

distributor's gross receipts: All gross income received by the distributor from the sub-distributor and/or theatre after deductions of all advertising, shipping costs, commissions and other costs. It is the gross income and represents the distributor's share. To confuse one even further it is also referred to as *net film rental*.

drive-in theatre: A theatre with no top and used exclusively for cars. There are approximately 5500 drive-in theatres in the U.S.A., averaging 550 cars per theatre.

DNU: This is the terminology used by theatres to indicate *Did Not Use*. This means that the theatre did not play the film. Alternate designations are DNP which means *Did Not Play*.

exhibitor: An exhibitor is the theatre playing the film.

first run-(premium)—key theatre: A picture which opens for the first time in a large city. Key theatre run is designed to advertise and create a feeling that this is a "big important picture" and is initially a set-up for normal multiple runs.

floating prints: These are release prints made by the film laboratory and are used to play multiples—one or more theatres—in the same town. These prints move from city to city and *float*.

in-house distribution: In this case, the distributor makes his own bookings directly with theatres. He performs all the functions of the sub-distributor including shipping prints, billing and collecting.

letter of credit-censor clause: In all foreign sales, the stipulation is made that the buyer must have approval from the local censor board before the deal is complete. The letter of credit can be invalid if the censor does not approve the motion picture to be shown in that foreign country.

M & E track: The music and effects track of the magnetic tape of the re-recording session. The M & E track is used in foreign sales where the purchaser wants to re-dubb the film and insert a foreign language. This technique allows the dialogue track to be mixed again with the M & E track for a new optical track and printing.

MPAA: The address of the Motion Picture Association of America is:

Motion Picture Association of America
522 Fifth Avenue,
New York, New York 10036

or

Motion Picture Association of America
8480 Beverly Blvd.
Los Angeles, California 90048

National Film Shippers: The address of the National Film Shippers is:

National Film Shippers
550 Main Street
Fort Lee, New Jersey 07024

one sheets: One sheets are displays used in motion picture theatre lobbies. They are usually 27 x 41 inches. Both the one sheets and inserts are taken from the art work on page one of the pressbook and reflect all key art.

optical track: This track is used by film laboratories in printing the answer print together with the cut negative. It is made from the magnetic track of the dubbed film and transferred optically to a negative track. On the release print, it is the thin jaggered line on the left side of the film and is referred to as *the sound track*.

pay television: The transmission of images and sound through the air, by cable, by wire or by any other means, systems or processors, whether or not now known or contemplated, to television receivers where reception is available only upon payment of a *per program charge*. This includes pay for view-television, subscription television, inflight television, and television for hotels, motels and hospitals.

playdate: This is a booking date made by a theatre to fit in to the schedule of films which the theatre will play. It is the time and date that the motion picture will play in his theatre and is reflected in booking reports.

players directory: A publication put out three times a year by the Motion Picture Arts and Sciences. It is for performing talent and production companies and first began in 1937. It lists over 8500 artists and their agents.

playing flat: A booking term used to indicate that the motion picture will be paid for at a flat rental. This is usually done when a motion picture is in its second run and plays *at the bottom of the bill*. This flat rental is paid regardless of whether the other companion motion picture made money or not.

playing percentage: A booking term used to, indicate that the motion picture will play *top of the bill* and will receive a percentage of the gross income received by the theatre. Minimum percentages are usually 25 percent of the net income of the theatre. The companion feature, which was booked *flat* receives its payment before any percentages are paid to the percentage film.

pressbook: This is a sales tool. It is a brochure of the motion picture which is used by the theatres to book the motion picture and to use the ads and publicity contained in the pressbook for local advertising, radio and television spots and newspapers. It also shows the *one sheets* which are available for sale.

PX: This is an abbreviation of the Armed Forces post exchanges.

Register of Copyright: Their address is as follows:
Register of Copyright
Copyright Office
Library of Congress
Washington, D.C. 20540.

release prints: These are prints which are manufactured by film laboratories after approval of the answer print. They are a combination of the action track (picture) and the sound track (optical). They are projected in theatres for audience viewing.

re-recording: This is the process whereby all the components of the cut film, together with sound components, i.e., dialogue, music and sound effects are combined onto one magnetic track onto an optical track which is developed as a negative by the film laboratory.

residuals: Residuals are payments made to artists for re-runs of television shows. Usually, only eight re-runs are considered in residual payments. Residuals are also paid for television commercials.

Screen Actors Guild: The address of the Screen Actors Guild is as follows:

Screen Actors Guild

7750 Sunset Blvd.

Hollywood, California 90046

second run-(Multiple run): When multiple theatres participate in releasing the film at the same time and mutually share advertising costs. If the picture does not have a premium run, then it is called a *first run*.

sliding scale: This is an actuarial accounting process used by theatres to compute the amount of money due a distributor on a percentage playdate.

sub-distributor: An agent of the distributor who functions as the distributor in his own exchange or territory. He usually receives a 25 percent commission for his efforts. He books the motion picture into theatres in his exchanges.

sub-run (Pick ups): Sub-run follows the multiple run and takes advantage of previous publicity and exposure. Sub-run includes pick-up theatres not nessarily included in the multiple run, but could include some of the second run and multiple theatres.

trailer: This is a sales tool used by theatres to show coming attractions. A trailer is usually rented by the theatre through the distributor or his accessory house for a fee. The trailer is made from *A* and *B* negatives and from all sound units. It is re-recorded at a sound studio. A CRI is made for an answer print and subsequent release prints. There are usually two trailers made for each release print.

trailer tags: This is the designation made by the MPAA of the rating assigned. This rating must be on all trailers, pressbooks, one sheets and all advertising. It is called a *Tag* because it must accompany the trailer when shown in theatres.

U.S. Copyright Office: The address of this office is:
Copyright Office
The Library of Congress
Washington, D.C. 20540

90/10: An arrangement whereby the distributor receives 90 percent of the gross box office figures. The distributor pays the theatre a house allowance as well as all advertising and all costs incurred through the theatre exhibition.

Index

Index

Edited by Ellen A. Britsch